The Book of Names

an accounting of abortion's daily toll

Sylvia Dorham

dedication

for the 19,178 people who will die today from
chemical abortion,
a birth control "side-effect"

and

for Joshua,
who waits.

prelude

On Tuesday, April 5, 2011, a terrible tragedy occurred in the United States of America.

While news of the loss of the greatest resource — humanity — was not noted in any media outlet, the death of 3,877 citizens affected a great many people and permanently changed the course of the future on Earth.

The loss of American human life in a single, peacetime day was unparalleled in the history of the nation.

At least since Monday, April 4, 2011.

Abortion.

Perhaps the true impact of that single day's loss of life will never be fully understood, but to hear some of the victims' stories, to know what *might have been,* is to begin to comprehend what potential slipped from the hands of those who had a choice that day.

Each person, an irreplaceable life,
incomprehensibly connected to every other human.

Connected to you.

Here are the names of the 3,877 people who might have lived, had they not been aborted that day.

May they rest in peace.

A

Alfred - would have turned out to be a jerk. His mother, an eighteen-year-old soccer star impregnated by her coach will soon become one of the pioneers of women's soccer in the US, and he would have grown up under the half-star of her minor celebrity. Which is enough attention to ruin any child.

Drinking, drugging, petty crime, would have defined his existence. A life of supreme annoyance to his grandparents, with whom he would spend his time when not trying to live up to his mother's high standards of athletic performance.

So it's probably better the way it turned out.

Except that Alfred would have also played soccer, and although he would never reach his mother's heights of fame, he would have made a major league team and played for three years before a blown-out knee would sideline him.

He would have coached more than 2,200 young soccer players at the sport-intensive clinics he would have run in San Diego, from which, seventeen more major leaguers would have risen.

Of course, his foul mouth, which would never be tamed in spite of the general calming of spirit provided by the knee injury, would have gotten him in trouble with parents. Although he would have experienced relative satisfaction with his career, he would have divorced twice and only been able to see his three kids on alternate weekends.

Anola - would have been a preschool teacher. Her mother is a dropout, whose family of origin is comprised of a single mother and a grandmother. Neither are sober.

When Angela was conceived, the two generations in front of her were not in agreement about her future. She would have been the first of the them all to graduate from high school and receive an AA degree. She would have secretly loved a country music legend, although she would settle for a guy she would meet at Wendy's after the game one Friday. Armed with her degree in early childhood education, Anola would have taught at Forestwood Elementary School in the pre-school classroom for seven years before having children of her own. She would have stayed home to care for them and her aging mother while her husband deployed with the Air Force.

She would have died at sixty-one in an automobile crash, survived by two girls, seven grandkids, her husband, and her aged mother.

Anika - would have been a foster parent. At age fourteen, she would have become friends with a girl in her class who lived with a foster-family.

They would have taught her the beauty and struggle of working with children from difficult backgrounds. She would have studied social work in college until she dropped out and stayed home to have babies with Trey. Soon, they would discover their infertility. They would have discussed the possibility of taking in kids, and he wouldn't like it. She would have pointed out the money they would be paid if they did, and he would have changed his mind. Together, they would have sheltered forty-one children over the course of the next twenty-seven years before Anika would decide to move to Florida to be near her parents. Trey would pass away ten years later in a boating accident, and Anika would write their memoirs.

The foster kids and their children would have had the tremendous gift of stability, which she helped plant in their upheaved lives.

Angel - would always want to change his name. When his illegal immigrant mother would try to teach him the beauty of it, he would remind her that in the US, it sounded like a girl's name. He would grow up conversational in his native Spanish, but his children would not be able to communicate with their family in El Salvador when he would bring them there on his thirty-seventh birthday. Both children, fully integrated into American culture, would be horrified and scared by the standard of living in Central America, something even Angel didn't remember.

One would return home and a decade later, arrange for a doctor to visit the small village of his ancestors. The doctors would help cure a little child carrying a virulent bacteria, averting an epidemic which could have left twenty percent of the population blind.

Anton - would have sung. His short life, highlighted by Downs Syndrome, would have been measured in surgeries, therapies, and wheelchairs.

His love for music would have inspired and brought to tears anyone who heard him sing. His four year and three month life span would have taught four future teachers not to fear children with disabilities.

It also would give his mother a lasting joy to remember through the pain of his death.

She would have spoken about him often in the next quarter-century, and her words would give courage to thirteen other mothers with poor prenatal diagnoses, giving them the courage to let their babies live.

Angela - Would have three girls, two dogs, a husband and raise bees.

Angelina - Would meet and marry her husband on subsequent Valentine's days. Their seven children, thirty-seven grandchildren, and one-hundred eleven great-grands would call her 'Nonna.' She would live to be ninety-seven.

Annabelle - would have lived her life in service of books. A librarian and school principal, there would not have been a day in her life which passed without the company of books. She would encourage several generations of readers who passed through St. William Middle School in the days before she became principal. Even in the latter role, Annabelle would continue to encourage students to read by rewarding good behavior with books.

Antonio - A building engineer, 'Tonyo' would have been a loyal Steelers fan. He would maintain four different buildings and gain too much weight before a heart attack would take him from his brothers and sister at age forty-eight.

Alice - a suburban socialite, Alice would have had those long legs that make a girl fashionable everywhere, especially at poolside parties. Leukemia would take her before her college loans were paid off, saddling her grieving parents with $73,000 in promissory notes.

Andrew - Orange County, New York's only two-time National Inner-Tubing Champion, Andrew would drive a propane delivery truck and a snow-plow, which would have made him a favorite at the Yoho Cafe where the parking lot is particularly large. He would have married young, been addicted to pornography, and divorce after two affairs.

Amy - Genes would have been the bane of Amy's life, bad acne and a pudgy belly tying her to her family of origin. Amy would have started a life-long diet at age seven, and still be secretly binging when she died at eighty-two.

Adam - Growing up in a small town in northern Colorado, Adam would have enjoyed winter sports and engines. Even after a stint in the Navy and a job at a crank shop in Texas, Adam would always return to the snowy mountains where a drunken snowmobile accident would eventually claim his life.

Abraham - Political life would be the logical solution for this tall young man with a patriot's name, but Abraham's career choices were limited by severe rheumatoid arthritis, which left him wheelchair-bound. Never one to take a set back personally, Abraham would have created a new computer language which would be used extensively to program medical mobility devices for the disabled.

Aurelia - a flute player in high school, Aurelia would have enjoyed classical music all her life, taking her daughter all the way to New York City to hear a world-class flautist perform at Carnegie Hall. Aurelia's daughter would have hated her, and family gatherings would have been particularly trying until a grandson would be born whose musical genius would unite all three generations.

Angie - petite and hard of hearing, Angie would have utilized her organizational skills by making databases for the US Geological Survey.

Andromeda - daughter of world class scientists, would have frittered her life away with destinationless travel and a collection of boyfriends.

Ado - son of an American mother and a Japanese father, he would have learned both languages fluently, and become a business ambassador for three large corporations seeking to do business abroad. His travel schedule would have caused him to miss his daughter's ballet debut in fourth grade, science fair in eighth grade, and college graduation. He would be confined to a nursing home at sixty-three for early-onset Alzheimer's Disease.

These people also died that day. What could have been?

Aubrey Alaina Abbie Andy Andrew
Abbott Abby Abigail Abilene Abrianna
Alana Alanis Alexa Alistair Albert
Aldan Alec Alexander Alicia Alegra
Amos Allie Amor Analise Anastasia
Amanda Arsenio Apria Apple Aqua
Archibald Archer Ansel Antoine Ansley
Anya Ashlyn Arthur Artie Arvin
Ashlee Ashleigh Ashlyn Augustine Autumn
Ava Avani Ave Avery Aviana
Avis Avon Alpine Alexander Althea
Alvaro Alvin Alvis Amable Amadeus

Amadi Amal Amancio Annie Anna
Anne Anne Anna Ana Anthony
Arius Arizona Arjan Arlene Arleen
Armand Aramelle Arnie Arnold Arnoldo
Aaron Arne Armando Arlanna Arius
Arlo Aravis Amal

Total: 106

B

Baird - in third grade, Baird would have had an art teacher who taught him the rudiments of technical drawing. His artist father, if he had stayed around, would have recognized the budding talent in his son. His mother would have encouraged her son's talent with drawing pads and pencils for his birthdays. Baird's drawings of "exploded" machines would have become standard in engineering manuals and textbooks.

Bonnie - a wealthy woman from Marblehead, Bonnie would have checked all the boxes a young Millenial needed. Designer preschool, elementary enrichment, prep school, an Ivy League university, but her distant parents and lack of role model would cause her to bounce from relationship to relationship and job to job, trying to find something to fill the hole in her heart.

Buster - the name on his birth certificate would have read "George" after his maternal great-grandfather, but his grandmother liked the way 'Buster' rolled off her tongue. He would have been a big man, barely squeezing behind the wheel of the classic Thunderbird he rebuilt in his teens. His mother and sister would have relied on him for transportation and the security they will never know. His grandmother would have raised him, and she would have known the comfort of his company during his grandfather's slow deterioration with Parkinson's Disease.

Barbie - would have been accepted at her father's college alma mater the day he succumbed to kidney cancer. Her mother would have harassed her about her weight.

Bella - living up to her name, Bella would have been beautiful. Her ringlet curls and soft, smooth skin would have been well worth a difficult pregnancy for her mother. She would have been a little spoiled by her maternal grandparents, but would have made Eric an excellent wife and Jaileene an excellent mother.

Betsy - anxious to escape the cycle of drugs and abusing men, would have left her mother's home early to fend for herself. Rooming with friends, she would have worked hard to avoid her mother's lifestyle, taking refuge in her sister's church. Eventually, she would have become a store manager and raised her children and their dog in relative peace.

Bob - an electrician, Bob would have been an average student with average interests. His free time would be mostly devoted to video games, and on weekends he would hang out with his buddies at one of their houses well into his thirties and his second marriage.

Benjamin - growing up in a suburban home, the son of a high-school girl and her boyfriend, Benjamin would himself have married his high-school sweetheart and had two sons. One would have become a Navy SEAL and be killed in a combat training exercise, and the other would commute three hours to work at a lighting manufacturer. Benjamin's granddaughter would have been an endocrinologist.

Bill - showing promise in every sport he touched, his status-conscious mother would have been certain to enroll him in community teams every season of the year. He would enter the military and play inter-company sports until a rotator cuff injury would stop him.

Billy - preferring to be alone, Billy would have hidden from other kids in the adult sections of the library. Since no one at home wanted him, he would hang out by himself or at his next door neighbor's. He would have taken a job as a landscaper for a housing development and worked there for thirty-seven years, retiring at a small party he didn't plan to attend, except that a co-worker's wife insisted.

These people, too, died that day. Who is being killed right now?

Baba   Baby   Babette   Baden   Bai
Bailey   Bairn   Baker   Baldwin   Ballard
Bambi   Bambina   Bandele   Banner Bernard

Barak   Barbra   Barbara   Barb   Barb
Barclay   Barnabas   Barney   Baron   Bart
Bartholomew   Barton   Baruch   Barry Bessie
Basil   Baylee   Bea   Beatrice   Beatrix
Beau   Bebe   Bonita   Becca   Beckham
Behitha   Belo   Belinda   Bellisima   Belita
Belle   Ben   Benard   Benedetta   Benedict
Benevuto   Benicia   Benigno   Benita   Benjamin
Benjy   Bennett   Benny   Benson   Benvenuto
Bereniece   Berg   Berit   Berke   Bernadino
Bernardo   Bert   Berta   Beryl   Bess
Beth   Beth   Beth   Bethany   Betsy
Bettina   Betty   Beulah   Beverly   Beyonce
Bhuvan   Biagio   Bianca   Bibi   Bibiana
Bill   Billie   Billy   Billy   Bina
Black   Blade   Bjorn Bette Bishop
Blair   Blaire   Blaise   Blake   Blakeney
Blanca   Blaze   Blithe   Blossom   Blue
Blue   Bluma   Bly   Bo   Bobby
Bode   Bolivar   Bonaventura   Boniface   Bonita
Bono   Boone Boris   Borka   Boyce
Boyd   Brac   Brad   Bradley   Brady
Brandee   Branden   Brando   Brandy   Brady
Brasilia   Braun   Bray   Brianna   Brenda
Brenna   Brett   Bria   Brian   Brianne
Bridget   Brigham   Brigitte   Brita   Britney
Brittaney   Brock   Brody   Bronson   Brooke
Brooks   Brown   Bruno   Bryant   Bryce
Buena   Bubba   Buck   Buddy   Buffy
Bunny   Burke   Burt   Butch   Buzz
Byram   Byron   Bree   Bran   Bingham

Total: 180

C

Cayce - people are not evil. They are born good, but stained. If the stain is not washed off, other dirt begins to accumulate, and soon, as in Cayce's case, they are filled with darkness.

Cayce's mom is heavily involved with a ritualistic form of worship that includes in its practice the precursors to his conception. Had he lived, he too would have become involved in the rites, and he would have died at age seventeen after having impregnated three girls and murdering one.

Caleb - one of those people who just likes to please, Caleb would have smiled at everyone, but rarely moved off the couch unless his mother yelled at him. He would have married a woman just like her, after she convinced him it was time to tie the knot, and showed him what to do. Even at his wedding reception, you would have found him in a chair, smiling broadly at his bustling bride. His children, too, would tend to be happiest when sitting still, a fact which would have caused his wife no end of frustration. Caleb's great-great grandchild (there were only nineteen of them), ironically would have been a track star, earning the title of 'Fastest Man on Earth' two years in a row.

Channing - picture books of exotic destinations would have fed his childhood desire to travel to distant lands. He would have attended a boarding school in India for the children of diplomats and learned to love East Asian food. One of the few white men to visit one particular portion of rural Vietnam, he would have called international attention to the threat of counterfeit malaria medicine sold to the populace. Although he would have never married, his legacy would have been generations of disease-free children, twenty-one of whom would eventually receive an education through his memorial foundation.

Charlie - friends and brothers would have shaken their heads at the energy of the headstrong boy who would have been the youngest firefighter in the small town volunteer squad. At eighteen, he would have won 'Firefighter of the Year.' In his early twenties, he would have discovered his skill with horses and moved to a farm on the other side of the state to work at a ranch breeding race horses. He would have been the glue to hold his brothers together on the sudden deaths of his parents.

Charlotte - 'Char,' as she would have been known to her friends, would have been stuck in the same welfare-dependent state which has plagued her family for generations. Her ambition to teach Kindergarten would have been thwarted by early pregnancy following rape by one of her step-fathers. She would have opted to keep the baby, and while he and his children would die in their early twenties on the street, his grandchildren, Char's great-grands, would have found their way out of the city, received good educations, and lived stable lives. One of them, a physician, would have been the parent of the inventor of the AIDS vaccine.

Carlos - who would have been the father of five and the grandfather of twelve, would have spent a good deal of his early years standing at the day-laborer site near the Shell gas station, waiting to be hired. He would work hard on his English, and have a bad temper. In one rage, he would have injured his wife, who would walk with a limp for the rest of her life. One child and three of his grandchildren would have particularly touched his heart, and he would imbue them with his love of soccer. One would go on to play soccer in state championship games.

Cinta - a thin woman with long, black hair, Cinta would have been a physical therapist at a busy clinic, treating more than 3,000 patients a year for twenty-seven years. In her retirement, she would go on pilgrimage to religious sites throughout the country, leading a small group of women from her church.

Constancia - would have lived in fear of her mother, who was too young to be a good parent. She would have found refuge in the home of her grandmother, who would have loved her fiercely. Without legal custody of her estranged daughter's child, however, Constancia's grandmother would have had to go through an exhausting and expensive court proceeding before finally gaining custody of the child just shy of her third birthday. Constancia would work hard in every job she held and support her grandmother when spinal damage from a car accident prevented the grandmother from continuing to work.

Cappa - would have been a pretty girl with a crooked smile, the result of being bitten on the face by a dog in her toddlerhood. Cappa would have gone to work for the Postal Service in her early twenties. Sharp observational skills would have led her to report one of the largest waste, fraud, and abuse cases of the century. Her subsequent pay increase would have helped her buy the house in which she was killed when a gas line broke in the middle of the night.

These people died that day, too. Thank goodness you survived.

Cade   Cadenza   Cady   Cesar   Cailyn
Caine   Caitlyn   Cal   Caleb   Cayley
Calista   Calla   Callia   Callie   Calliope
Calvin   Cam   Camber   Camden   Cameron
Camila   Camille   Campbell   Can   Cambree
Candace Candelaria Candice Candida   Candie
Candy   Cannon   Canta   Capri   Cara
Caprice   Caralynn   Caressa   Carey   Caridad
Carina   Carissa   Carl   Carleigh   Carlen
Carllin   Carlita   Carlo   Carlos   Carlos
Carlotta   Carlton   Carly   Carlyn   Carmen
Carmela   Carmelita   Carmine   Carol   Carolina

Caroline Carolyn Caron Carrie Carson
Carsten Carter Carver Cary Cascada
Case Casey Cash Casimir Casper
Cassandra Cassia Cassidy Castel Cat
Catalina Cate Catherine Catherine Cathy
Catlin Cayden Cayenne Cayla Caylin
CeCe Cecelia Cecil Cecile Cecilia
Cecily Cedric Celeste Celia Celina
Celine Chad Chaim Chakra Chaela
Chan Chana Chance Chandler Chandra
Chanel Channah Chantal Chantel Chantoya
Chao Charisse Charissa Charity Charity
Charla Charleen Charlene Charles Charles
Charlette Charlotte Charlton Chas Chase
Chastity Chauncey Chavez Chava Chaya
Chelle Chelsea Chelsey Chen Cheng
Chenille Cher Cheree Cheri Cherie
Cherish Cherry Cheryl Chess Chester
Chet Chevelle Cheyenne Chi Chiara
Chica Chico Chill Chilton China
Chip Chiquita Chita Chitt Chiyoko
Chloe Cho Chole Chou Chris
Chrissy Christa Christabel Christian Christiana
Christina Christine Christopher Christos Christy
Chuck Chung Chuong Chynna Cian
Cicely Cicero Cicily Ciel Cielo
Cierra Cilicia Cindy Cirila Ciro
Cissy Citro Claire Clara Clare
Clarence Clarice Clarissa Clark Claude
Claudette Claudia Claudio Claus Clay
Clayton Clea Cleatus Clem Clement
Clemence Clemens Clementine Cleo Cleopatra
Cliff Clifton Clint Clio Clive

Clodagh   Cloris   Cloud Clover Clovis
Clyde Coby Cocheta CoCo   Cody
Coe   Coen   Coeur   Colby   Cole
Coleman   Colette   Colin   Colleen   Colin
Colman   Colt   Colton   Columbo   Conan
Conary   Concepcion   Cong   Conley   Connell
Conner   Connery   Connie   Connor   Conor
Conrad Conroy Consolata Consolacion Constance
Constantine Consuela Contessa Conway Cookie
Cooper   Cora   Coralita   Coraline   Corazon
Corbeau   Corbett   Corbin   Cordero   Coretta
Corey   Corin   Corina   Corinne   Corliss
Cormac   Cornelia   Cornell   Cort   Cortez
Corwin   Cory   Cosima   Cosma   Costa
Coty   Courtland   Courtney   Coyne   Craig
Crane   Crawford   Crayton   Creed   Creighton
Crecencia   Cricket   Crispin   Crista   Cristina
Cristobal   Cristofer   Cruz   Cruzita   Crystal
Cullen   Culver   Curran   Curt   Curtis
Cutler   Cutter   Cy   Cyanne   Cybil
Cynthia   Cyrene   Cyril   Cyrus   Czar
Cyndi

Total: 340

D

Devon - his life would have been normal, if that word can be applied to a unique, individual life with the flavoring and nuance brought to it by fresh perspective. It was his mother, whose life changed so dramatically at his death. She was a sensitive girl by nature, introspective, and prone to deep thoughts - all factors which attracted her to the poetic man with whom she would conceive a child. When he heard of Devon's existence, the poetic man beat her until she could no longer stand.

She managed to carry Devon into the second trimester in spite of the now regular beatings. Unable to process the situation, Devon's mother passed through life in a trance-like fog of fear. When the father of the baby forced her to the place where the baby would be 'taken care of,' it was her body that resisted. Unable to complete the procedure due to maternal hemorrhage, the clinic finally sent the dying mother to the hospital where her life was rescued at the last moment. Not, however, before she saw the remains of her son.

She remained in a catatonic state for several days. Social services was called when the marks of the beatings were discovered, but the perpetrator had disappeared back into the poetic world which spawned him.

Devon's mother's body healed in time.

Her mind has not. The image of her son's mangled body always before her, she takes two anti-depressants daily, and remains incapacitated during the four weeks prior to Mother's Day.

Delia - would have had bright red curly hair.

Dixie - her mother would have named this Northern girl in honor of her favorite song. Dixie, a dental hygienist, would have been called 'Dix' by her friends. Concerned the name did not sound professional enough, Dixie would have filled out forms using the name Wynn.

Dexter - highly coordinated, Dexter would have soldered components onto custom computer motherboards. A computer tech in every sense, his co-workers would have referred to him as 'Dec-tec.' His addiction to marijuana would lead to dabbling in 'harder' drugs which would eventually require a two month stay at a detox and treatment center. When he would leave, clean, he would redesign the program, creating several innovations to the detox process which would earn him acclaim and make his name well-known in the drug rehabilitation community.

Deborah - thick, long, black hair would have been her hallmark, but since she would wear it tightly wrapped behind her head, no one would notice its glossy beauty. The first time her fiancé would see it down, his intake of breath would be audible. From that day on, he would unclip it whenever they were together, and the hair would curl around him as they walked, enveloping them both. When they were married and had twin babies, Deborah would cut her hair to save time, but her husband would have grieved the loss and she would have grown it back just to please him.

David - unable to conceive his own children, David and his wife would have adopted two children from China. The sight of the orphanage in his children's country of origin would have so saddened him that he would have begun encouraging his friends and coworkers to adopt as well. The town in which he lived would have seen its population enriched by a total of twenty-seven children from the same orphanage. David's daughter would have returned to China in adulthood and herself adopted children.

Donna - would have been a chain smoker. Her house and children filthy, she would have enjoyed science fiction books more than some of the basic motherly tasks, and her children would be picked on at school for their dirty, smoke-smelling clothes.

Doreen - a popular, academically-gifted girl, Doreen would have been hit by a drunk driver one night, a week before her high-school graduation. Her small town would have reeled at the news and been drawn tightly together in support of her parents, and her twin brother. The school playground would have been renovated and dedicated in her honor.

Dora - her fine, blond hair unreliable, Dora would have worn it in a small bun and covered that with a hat. She would have worked in a hardware superstore and have been the first woman to have 'perfect attendance' at work for ten years straight.

Darin - would have been an Army armored cavalry driver. He would have served three tours in the war and written a wildly popular blog about his experiences. Every generation of his family from then on would have had an Army member in it.

These people also died that day. Some shared the same name and are listed twice.

Dacey   Dacia   Daffodil   Dahlia   Dai
Daichi   Daire   Daishiro   Daisy   Dakota
Dale   Dalia   Dalila   Dalinda   Dallas
Dallin   Dalton   Dama   Damara   Damaris
Dameka   Damian   Damien   Damon Diane
Damyan   Dan   Dana   Dana   Danae
Danby   Dane   Daniel   Daniel   Daniel
Danelle   Danesha   Danessa   Danette Dangela
Danica   Dania   Daniela   Danielle   Danika
Dana   Danny   Dante   Danya   Daphne
Daquan   Dara   Darby   Darcie   Darcy
Darda   Dareh   Daria   Darian   Dario
Darius   Darla   Darlene   Darlita   Darnell
Darrell   Darren   Darrius   Darryl   Darwin
Darya   Daryl   Dash   Daha   Dashiell

Dave   Dave   Daveigh   David   David
David   Davida   Davina   Davis   Davon
Dawn   Dawndrell   Dawson   Dax   Day
Daylin   Dayna   Dayshaun   Dayton Dylan
Deacon   Dean   Deana   Deandra   Deandre
Deangelo   Deanna   Debbie   Deborah   Debra
December   Decima   Decker   Dee   Deena
Deepak   Deidra   Deion   Dierdre   Deiter
Dejan   Dejanae   Del   Delaine   Delaney
Delano   Delfina   Delia   Delila   Dell
Della   Delores   Delphi   Delta   Demarco
Demarcus Demarion Demarius Demeter Demetra
Demetrius   Demi   Dempsey   Dena   Denae
Denham   Denis   Denise   Denisha   Denna
Dennis   Denny   Denton   Denzel   Denzel
Deo   Deon   Derby   Derek   Derica
Dermot   Deron   Derrick   Derry   Desdemona
Deserae Deshawn   Desiderio   Desiree Dessa
Destino   Destiny   Destry   Deus   Deva
Devan   Devaun   Deven   Devi   Devin
Devon   Dewey   Dewitt   Dex   Dexter
Dextra   Dezi   Dharma   Dhaval   Dhyana
Dia   Diamond   Diana   Diana   Diandra
Diara   Dick   Dido   Diedrick   Diego
Diem   Dierdra   Dieter   Dillan   Dillon
Dima   Dina   Dino   Dior   Dirk
Diva   Divya   Dixon   Dmitri   Demetri
Doherty   Dolly   Dolores   Dom   Dominic
Dominica   Dominique   Don   Donae   Dyson
Donahue Donald   Donata   Donatello   Dong
Donnel   Donnelly   Donnica   Donnie   Donovan
Dorcas   Dore   Dori   Doria   Dorian
Dorie   Doris   Dorotea   Dorothy   Dory

Dot Dotty Doug Douglas Dove Doyle Draco Dragon Drake Drea Drew Driver Drogo Drury Duane Duarte Dubois Dude Duena Duke Dulce Dulcina Dumi Duncan Dung Dunn Durand Dustin Dusty Dutch Duyen Dwayne Dwight Dyan Duy Dylan Diane

Total: 285

E

Evan - an only child, Evan would have grown up in the company of his academically-inclined mother, grandmother, and grandfather. Exploring mathematical equations and relationships would have been part of his daily experience, and it would be no surprise when he became an astronomer. Three Ph.Ds later, Evan would be ensconced in an astrophysics lab at an expensive university where he would formulate several theories about the origin of the universe, and discover a new class of particles. His discoveries would gave affected space station design and deep space exploration for the next three generations.

E'latay - the seventh child of an illiterate inner city mother and her drug-dealing john father would have been born addicted to crack cocaine and suffering from the effects of fetal alcohol syndrome. Found on the street at age three-weeks next to her unconscious mother, E'latay would have been hospitalized, then placed in foster care. Adopted, E'latay would have suffered from severe behavioral and cognitive disabilities, causing her adoptive family to spend much of the ensuing eighteen years in doctors' offices and therapy. They would come out more patient and humbler than when they started. E'latay would have lived in a group work/live home, heavily medicated for the rest of her life.

Enrique - the son of the wild child in a minister's family, he would have grown up in Church on Sundays and Wednesdays. He would have developed a love for the Holy Bible and gone to seminary after high school. Training to be a missionary, Enrique would have traveled around the United States, preaching and teaching in rural Evangelical churches. He would have married and had a daughter and two sons. The child of his second son would have been a prominent televangelist.

Eppie - A quiet child, Eppie would have loved the out-of-doors. Summers away from her city home at the home of an aunt in the country would have solidified her love of solitude. She would have started an organic farm and done most of the labor herself, hiring out the marketing and business aspects of the enterprise. When a falling tree limb would crush her right leg, she would continue to work the farm in a brace. Unable to continue, she would develop a system of farming techniques for the disabled farmer.

Ed - son of a young enlisted military man and his girlfriend, Ed would have been raised everywhere his father was stationed. His parents precipitous marriage would have created the instability which caused Ed to develop a hot temper. He would be arrested for first degree assault before his twenty-first birthday and do jail time. Released and in therapy, Ed would begin competing in triathlons and eventually earn a coveted invitation to the Hawaii Triathlon where he would place twenty-third. He would have made his way into forestry and be killed while fighting a forest fire.

Etona - a social butterfly, Etona would have been petite and a little chubby.

Elizabeth - The oldest of three daughters, she would have learned leadership early and gone on to teach school. After seven years in the classroom, Elizabeth would have moved into administration, influencing more than 17,000 children over thirty-two year career as principal. Her policies and methods would have been used in schools throughout the nation to encouraged higher performance from teachers and students alike. On her death from breast cancer, a school of education at the State College would be named in her honor.

These people also died that day. More people than you have on your contacts list.

Eamon   Earl   Earleen   Earvin   Easton
Ebbe   Eben   Ebony   Ebony   Echo
Edana   Eddie   Eden   Edena   Edgardo
Edie   Edith   Edmund   Eduoard   Eduardo
Eduarte   Edward   Efrain   Eileen   Eire
Ekaterina   Elaine   Elaina   Elana   Elden
Eleanor   Eleazar   Electra   Elena   Elgin
Eliada   Eliakim   Eliam   Elias   Elie
Elijah   Elinor   Eliot   Elisa   Elisabeth

Elisaveta   Elise   Elisha   Elissa   Elita
Eliud   Eliza   Elizabeth   Elizabeth   Elkanah
Ella   Ellen   Elliana   Ellie   Elliot
Elliott   Ellis   Ellison Elmer   Elsa
Elsbeth   Elspeth   Elton   Elvis   Eli
Elyse   Emanuel   Emanuele   Ember   Emerald
Emerson   Emery   Emil   Emile   Emilia
Emiliana   Emiliano   Emilie   Emilio   Emily
Emlyn   Emma   Emma   Emmalee   Emmalyn
Emmeline   Emmet   Emmy   Emory   Ena
Ender   Engel   Enid   Ennio   Ennis
Enrico   Enrique   Enya   Eoin   Epiphany
Ephraim   Epifanio   Eracio   Erasto   Eric
Erica   Erika   Erik   Erin   Erma
Ermengarde   Ernest Ernesto   Ernesto   Eros
Errol   Ervin   Erwin   Esma   Esme
Esmeralda Esperanza Essence Esteban Estee
Estefania   Estela Estella   Estelle   Ester
Etania   Etan   Ethan   Ethel   Etienne
Etoile   Etta   Euclid   Eugene   Eunice
Eustace   Eva   Evan   Evana   Evander
Evangeline   Eve   Evelyn   Evera   Everett
Evette   Evie   Evia   Evita   Evonne
Evony   Ewan   Ezra   Eytan   Ezekiel
Eligio

Total: 173

F

Fredrick - would have always been called Freddy, although he would hate the name and the way people would tease him about Freddy Krueger, the terrifying movie villain. At fourteen, a freshman in high school, Fredrick would have taken a computer animation course as an elective. The class would change his life and steer him toward his career in animation. With his creative streak, he would have invented three new animated made-for-TV movies, one of which would have become a classic Christmas special.

Fredrick would have subsisted on ramen noodles and energy drink, a diet occasionally punctuated by sushi and french fries. Warned by a doctor to improve the quality of his food intake and to get some exercise, he would have become a mediocre bicyclist.

Frances - would have loved sculpting and attended the Rhode Island School of Design. Her fashion sense, artistic ability, and a random encounter with an auto manufacturer at a car trade show, where she would have been with her boyfriend, would have led to a career in automobile model making. She would have suffered the loss of a seven-year-old daughter to cancer, and have been overprotective with her other two children.

Fiona - would have loved romance novels, sneaking them into the cubicle where she would have worked as a medical secretary. Fairly happy in her marriage, Fiona would be surprised and devastated to learn of her husband's addiction to pornography. Out of fear for the safety of her girls, she would have left him for four years, until he conquered the demon and came to re-propose. After they were back together, Fiona would no longer need romance novels to feel loved.

Franklin - would have been adopted at age six-hours. Growing up in a stable, mid-western home would have been something he would have taken for granted, and it wouldn't be until meeting his birth mother in the middle of his twenty-third year that he would realize just how lucky he had been. Franklin would have had six children, thirteen grands, and thirty-four great-grands, each generation with a representative on the police force.

Farrah - with long, feathered hair, would have run cross-country track at boarding school as child. She would earn certification as an athletic trainer and spend eighteen years as a track and cross-country coach with one state and three regional championships to her credit.

Faith - would have lived up to her name. An early interest in religious life would have led her to discover her calling to be a Franciscan nun. On the day of her first religious vows, her mother would have fallen and badly broken her knee. During the ensuing years of pain, Faith would live at home to care for her mother. When her mother died suddenly from a blood clot after knee-replacement surgery, Faith would finally be able to live full-time with her religious sisters.

These people also died that day. While we were drinking our coffee.

Fabian   Fabiana   Fabio   Fadey   Fahima
Fai   Falcon   Falk   Fancy   Fannie
Fantasia   Farley   Fateh   Fatima   Fatima
Faustine   Fauve   Fawn   Fawzi   Fay
Faye   Fayre   Fedele   Federico   Felice
Felicia   Felicity   Felipe   Felix   Felton
Femke   Fenton   Ferdinand   Fergie Fernan
Fergu   Fern   Fernando   Ferris   Fia
Fiana   Fico   Fidel Fidelio   Fifi
Filia   Fina   Fineen   Finley   Findlay
Finnegan   Fiorello   Fiorenza   Fisher Fyodor
Fitzgerald   Fitzwilliam   Flan   Flann   Flannery
Flash   Flavia   Flavian   Felming   Fletcher
Fleur   Flint   Flip   Florence   Flora
Florian   Florissa   Floyd   Flynn   Forbes
Ford   Forrest   Forrester   Fortuna   Fortuo
Foster   Fraley   Fran   Francesca   Francisco
Franco   Francois   Frank   Franz   Fraser
Frederica   Freeman   Freida   Fremont   Frey
Frida   Fritz   Fumiko   Fynn

Total: 105

G

Gunther - a tightly wrapped umbilical cord would have caused trauma at his birth. All his life, Gunther would suffer the effects of those three minutes of insufficient oxygen reaching his brain. Developmentally delayed, he would have found the world frustrating and inhospitable. Anger would have built resentment and come out in frequent rage-filled fits until by chance he would experience the ocean alone in a small craft. The size and changeable nature of the sea, its fits and rages would have spoken to Gunther and he would have spent the rest of his life circumnavigating the world. Stopping to work in various ports to earn enough money to continue his perpetual voyage, he would have died at age fifty-three from food poisoning in Indonesia.

Gregory - a disappointment because of his existence, Gregory would have spent his life consciously and unconsciously trying to please his Dad. From a line of hunters and sportsmen, Gregory would have preferred to teach philosophy. He would have had to fund his own education and live in a tiny attic apartment until he finished his Ph.D. and could be hired at the university. His dissertation would have discussed the nature of relations between man and beast. His own son and daughter would have been of like-minded temperament, but his stepson's athletic build and cavalier attitude would have caused Gregory's feelings of inadequacy to surface, and the two would never get along.

Gillian - would have had it all. She would be striking, if not beautiful, dress well, never want for money, and be raised by adoptive parents who would love her. Her calm demeanor and quiet humor would have won her deep-thinking friends. She would have started two foundations and served as chairman and spokeswoman for both, a life which would exhaust her and eventually lead to a health breakdown. Retiring to the seaside, she would spend the rest of her days in a seasonal resort town writing and wondering.

Georgiana - her English-major mother would have named her after the tall sister of Fitzwilliam Darcy in Jane Austen's Pride and Prejudice when the nurses would have measured her birth length at two inches longer than average. Consigned to daycare, extended care, and hundreds of camps during her childhood, Georgiana would develop a public persona which differed greatly from her interior state. At twenty-one, she would have discovered Teresa of Avila and learn about contemplative prayer. Her healing would have inspired three generations at her church, where she would speak frequently on the subject.

Grace - had she survived, would have loved Irish dance. Somewhat clumsier than the other girls in the class her grandmother would have paid for her to attend, she would have compensated with heart. Never much of a performer, she would have made a sizable nest egg in her computer career and raised her girls to love dance as well as patronize local dance theater. Her daughters would also teach their children to love dance, and Grace's dreams of elegant performance would have been realized in her grandson and great-granddaughter, each of whom would capture international attention for their skill and grace.

Granita - would have never had weekends off. Her mother was a manager and her father a server in the restaurant industry, and they would have opened a busy cafe in the heart of New Orleans where Granita would have spent the majority of her time until her own early marriage to a server in her parents' restaurant. She would eventually suffer the effects of second-hand smoke and move to a cottage in Maine, where the clearer air would help her stay alive until age sixty-seven.

Giles - would have served in the Marine Corp as part of a forward-deployed unit. On patrol one night, Giles would have taken a brick to the face while covering the retreat of his squad. He would die the next week from hidden bleeding in his brain. The three men of his squad would each name a child after him.

Greta - a horsewoman, Greta would start as a stable hand in her early teens and work her way up to owner of an Arabian breeding stable. Fierce and temperamental, she would have befriended animals much faster than humans. Marrying a heavy drinker for his connections in the industry, she would become crankier as she aged until only her expertise kept her socially solvent.

These people also died that day. Choose on name to linger over, and imagine how they might have affected you.

Gabby Gabe Gabriel Gabriela Gabrielle Gada Gael Gaetano Gage Gaia Gail Gaius Gala Galahad Galatea Gale Galen Galeno Galina Gallagher Galvin Gamma Gandhi Gannon Garima Gardenia Gardner Gareth Garfield Garin Garland Garnet Garren Garrett Garrick Garrison Garry Garson Garth Garth Garvey Gary Gasha Gaspard Gaston Gates Gaura Gauri Gavan Gavin Gabino Gavril Gayle Gazelle Geet Geir Gella Gemi Gemma Gene Genero Generosa Genesis Geneva Genevieve Genna Genova Gent Gentry Geoff Geoffrey Geona George Georgette Georgia Georgie Georgina Geovany Gerald Geraldine Geraldo Gerard Geri Gerianne Gerlinde Germain Germaine German Geronimo Gerry Gershom Gertrude Ghada Ghazi Ghita Gia Giacomo Giada Giancarlo Gianna Gianni Gibson Gideon Gidget Gift Gigi Gil Gilad Gilbert Gilberto Gilda Gilead Gili Gillespie Gillis

Gilmore   Gilroy   Gina   Ginger   Ginny
Gino   Gioia   Giorgio   Giovanna   Giovanni
Giselle   Gita   Gitano   Gitel   Giulia
Giuliana   Giulio   Giuseppe   Giustina   Giverny
Giza   Gizela   Gizi   Gladys   Glaucio
Glen   Glenda   Glenn   Glenna   Glennis
Glinda   Glison   Glora   Gloria   Gloriann
Glory   Glynn   Glynnis   Godana   Godelieve
Godfrey   Godfried   Godiva   Godwin   Golda
Goldie   Gomer   Gonzalo   Gopi   Gordon
Gordy   Gore   Goren   Goro   Gov
Gowan   Gracelyn   Gracie   Graciela   Gradin
Grady   Graeme   Graham   Gram   Granger
Grant   Granville   Gratian   Gray   Grayson
Grayton   Grazia   Greco   Greer   Gregg
Gregory   Gresham   Greta   Gretchen   Gretel
Grey   Greyson   Griffin   Griet   Grian
Griffith   Grisel   Grosvenor   Grover   Gruffudd
Gryphon Guadalupe Guadalupe   Guang   Guido
Guildford Guillaume Guillermo Guinevere   Gauri
Gulliver   Gury   Gunnar   Gunner   Guri
Gus   Gustave   Gustavo   Guthrie   Guy
Gwen   Gwendolyn   Gwyneth   Gwyneth
Gypsy

Total: 238

H

Hans - most folk are just ordinary folk. They're born, they live, they die. History closes around them like water around a pebble falling into a lake. Few make more impact. But Hans would have.

A brilliant military commander and inventor, he would have been home-schooled and steeped in history and science. His near-photographic memory would present him with factual information he had read since beginning to absorb military history and astronomy books at age three. Joining the military at age eighteen after completing his Master's degrees in Strategic Planning and Astrophysics, Hans would have quickly advanced to the rank of Lieutenant General, acting as military consultant to the Commander in Chief. Several timely decisions and strategic use of resources would have made him well known, but his discovery and promulgation of light-speed travel for military purposes would have made him a household name. The mechanisms of super-photaic flight would be named for him, establishing his legacy for succeeding generations.

Holly - the fourth girl in a suburban family, would have been different. Her quick wit, foresight, and intelligence would have given her the tools to manage early motherhood and a life of working for the state government. Her sisters would have dealt poorly with life and passed away relatively young, leaving Holly to care for their aging parents. She would have made a point of mailing holiday cards, greeting cards, birthday cards, and 'thinking of you' cards, just to remind people how much she cared.

Horatio - a surveyor, would have spent his adult life in an orange safety vest, measuring land and charting topography. A fan of college basketball, he would have a perfect bracket one year, earning him nearly $2,000 in his office pool.

Honey - a Flathead indian from a Montana reservation, Honey would have been educated in a Jesuit school and worked in Missoula. She would live to see her great-great-grandchildren, who wouldn't care much. A biographer would write her memoirs, bringing more attention to the perpetually downtrodden situation of her people.

Henry - would have become one of three janitors in a small rural school. An established bachelor, Henry would have surprised everyone - most of all himself - by marrying and having three children, all of whom would go to college.

Honario - would have never lived up to his name. Involved in gang activity from his earliest childhood memory, he would pass through puberty in a fog of drug-induced alter-consciousness until an altercation in a public park would lead to his death via gunshot wound. Three people would have witnessed his death, including an eight-year-old boy who would have never been able to forget it.

Harry - an aspiring actor, Harry would have supported his career with part-time jobs as a bouncer, restaurant server, coffee barista, package handler, and fast-food cook. When Harry would finally marry, it would be to a strong-willed, passionate woman who believed in nine-to-five jobs. Harry would no longer aspire to acting, but would become an accountant with a flair for Karaoke.

These people also died that day. One might have been your child's spouse.

Haben   Habiki   Hachiro   Hada   Hadassah
Hadley   Hadria   Haile   Hailey   Haines
Hajra   Hakan   Hal   Halden   Haley
Hall   Hallan   Halle   Hallie   Ham
Hamako   Hamal   Hamilton   Hamish   Hamlet
Hamlin   Hammer   Hammond   Hampton   Hana
Hanae   Hanako   Hanh   Hanley   Hanna
Hannah   Hansel   Hao   Haracha   Haranu
Harding   Hardy   Harlan   Harlean   Harley
Harlow   Harmon   Harmony   Harold   Haroun
Harper   Harriet   Harris   Harrison   Hart
Haruka   Haruko   Harvey   Hasad   Hassan
Hattie   Havana   Haven   Havily   Hawa
Hawk   Hayden   Hayes   Hayley   Hayward
Hazel   Heath   Heather   Heaton   Hebe
Hector   Hedda   Hedy   Hedya   Heidi

Heinrich   Heisman   Helaine   Helen   Helena
Helene   Helga   Heller   Helmfried   Hendrik
Henley   Henri   Henrietta   Henriette   Henrik
Hera   Herb   Herbert   Heremon   Herman
Heriberto   Hermione   Hernan Hernando   Hero
Herschel   Hertz   Hesper   Hessa   Hetty
Hewitt   Hezekiah   Hidalgo   Hideaki   Hidi
Hien   Hiero   Hilaire   Hilario   Hilary
Hilda   Hillary   Hilliard   Himani   Hina
Hiraku   Hiram   Hiroko   Hiroshi   Hoang
Holbrook   Holden   Hollace   Holland   Holleen
Hollis   Holt   Homer   Hong   Honor
Hope   Horace   Horst   Hosea   Hosei
Houston   Howard   Howe   Howell   Howie
Hubert   Huck   Hudd   Hudson   Hue
Huey   Hugh   Hugo   Humbert   Humberto
Hume   Hummer   Humphrey   Hung   Hunter
Huntley   Huong   Hussein   Huy   Hy
Hyacinth   Hyman

Total: 179

I

Indira - one of the first traits her mother would have noticed would have been Indira's quiet watchfulness. She would have listened carefully, and watched closely the faces of the adults around her. As she grew, her mother would have noticed the comforting, open silence with which Indira listened. It would not surprise her mother when the child's friends would come crying to to her and leave seemingly comforted. Her listening skills would have brought solace to others all Indira's long life.

Isabel - would have been the first grandchild in a wealthy Mexican family prominent in the greater Atlanta community. She would have been pampered and spoiled, respecting only those she considered her equal in socio-economic standing. Isabel would have found her niche in leadership of non-profit organizations, excelling in fundraising efforts and gala events. Her four children would have enjoyed the same benefits in life, and her grandchildren would have led the local nightlife scene. One great-grandchild would have founded a library in the family name, and two others would have established telecom businesses throughout North America.

Igraine - would have sold Mary Kay cosmetics. She never would have earned the car, but her diligent work would have won the grudging respect of her husband, who would have eventually been willing to pass out her business cards to his buddies at the factory, in case their wives were interested.

Ignatio - would have invented a new marketing technique which involved a virtual salesman being projected into busy hallways and corridors of major buildings, personally engaging individuals and inviting them into stores and distributing coupons. He would have been equally lauded and hated by the populace.

Immanuelle - would have spent twenty years as a flight attendant. As a child, she would have enjoyed serving cookies at the Christmas party, and trying to turn her mother's drinking binges into an elegant occasion - if only in her mind. The survival techniques she learned as the child of an alcoholic would help her deal with the increasingly anxious public on her flights in a post-9/11 world.

Indiana - would own two stetsons and a bullwhip, just to make people laugh. On dress-down days, he would wear them to work, as long as he didn't have any sales meetings. 'Indie' would have loved NASCAR and baseball.

Ice - would have been a better-than-average athlete without enough physical genius to propel him to the big leagues. He would have signed only two autographs, and eventually realized he needed a day job. Several years of study would give him a Physical Therapy degree, and Ice would stay in shape without having to pay for a gym membership by using the exercise machines in the office after hours. He would have enjoyed the giddy reactions of his aging female patients to his physical presence, and in the end, be pleased with his accomplishments. His son would have played on a league team where Ice would have tended the wounded.

These people also died that day. Where were they buried?

Ian   Ianna   Ibis   Ichiro   Ida
Idalee   Idalia   Idana   Ide   Idra
Iggi   Ignatius   Ike   Ilana   Ilaria
Iliana   Ilka   Illias   Ilona   Ilse
Ily   Ilya   Ilyssa   Imagine   Imala
Imani   Imelda   Imogen   Imri Izzy
Ina   Incenio   Independence   India Izumi
Indigo   Indra   Inez   Inga   Ingrid
Inigo   Inna   Inocencia   Integra   Ioan
Iola   Iolana   Iolani   Iolanthe   Iono
Iona   Ioviano   Ira   Iram   Ireland
Iren   Irena   Irene   Irina   Iris
Irish   Irma   Irving   Irwin   Isaac
Isaac   Isabella   Isadora   Isadore Iyana
Isaiah   Isaias   Isandro   Isha   Ishana
Ishiko   Ishmael   Isi   Isidore   Isidro
Isla   Ismaela   Ismet   Isolde   Isra
Israel   Issay   Itachi   Italia   Ithaca
Itsuki   Ivailo   Ivan   Ivana   Ivar

Ives   Ivette   Ivie   Ivo   Ivory
Ivria   Ivy

Total: 109

J

Jackson - would have been the second son of a military couple whose father was often at sea for extended periods of time. Unable to manage one child, his mother could not fathom having another with her husband away. Indeed, life would have been difficult for Jackson, his older brother, and his mother. But things would have worked out. A friend from a previous duty station would have moved in next door and provided Jackson's mother with the support she needed, and the two of them would have enrolled their children in the same classes and joined many of the same activities. Jackson would have been a happy child, always laughing and ready to make friends with anyone. When his father died overseas, it would have been Jackson who introduced his mother to the man she would marry, an accountant widower with a son of his own. But that's not the way it turned out.

Jerrie - a single mom, the child of her own single mom, Jerrie would have had little to do with 'normal' family life, instead living as a houseparent at a boarding school for diplomatic children whose parents were overseas on unaccompanied tours. She would have provided a modicum of stability for the children who knew their parents were in harm's way, and she would have had a talent for making any group of children feel like they belonged to each other. She would have held girls who had just learned of their parent's passing, she would have helped pack the belongings of joyful kids whose parents had been reassigned Stateside. Jerrie would have dealt with the emotional stress by overeating and going to daily Mass, and would have always been twenty pounds overweight.

Jeremy - in perpetual trouble at school, this short, stout Irishman would have gone on to be the head of a local drug ring in his minuscule community. His murder would have shocked the area and been the cause of whispers and rumors long after his two daughters would have left their "we miss you, daddy" signs on his grave.

Jill - a drifter and rebel, Jill would have had a shock of blond hair and a propensity for cracking her knuckles. Eventually marrying her long-term, live-in boyfriend, she would have struggled to have children of her own. They would adopt, divorce, get back together, and live in relative peace together until she would die at age forty-seven from an untreated infection in her foot, wounded on a rusted metal piling at the beach.

Joey - would have designed posters and bumper stickers. A flair for creating short, pithy sayings plus a working knowledge of computer graphics would have made it possible for him to make a living wage, once his wife took over the accounting.

James - A talker from the day he was born, James' mother would have wished for peace and quiet more times than she could count. He would have grown up always leading around a group of kids, and talking his way out of trouble. Politics would have been a natural outlet for James' skills, but two misdemeanors and a felony would have kept him from running for office. He would have learned much from his incarceration, however, and gone on to a career as a prison warden for some of the largest prisons in Arizona.

Jamondo - conceived at a party Jamondo's mother doesn't remember, the child would have grown up in poverty, raised primarily by his older sister. His presence would have helped her stay sane through the long, lonely days and nights when their mother was absent and there was no one in the apartment. Jamondo's sister would have made him baked beans from a can, and accidentally burned his chest and leg when he was three. The apartment manager would have heard his screams and called the police, who in turn would have involved social services.

A distant relative of the children would have come forward to take them, and they would have moved far from California, and spent the rest of their childhood in therapy. They would have struggled with behavior and mental health issues all their lives, and Jamondo would have required medication to stay stable, but both children would have been able to have families of their own and lived to enjoy grandchildren. Jamondo, at six feet, three inches and three hundred pounds would have protected his family fiercely, and cheered loudly at football games where his grandkids were playing. One grand-niece would have become the mayor of her town, passing several good (and a few poor) laws to protect children in foster care.

These people also died that day. Who are their mourning families?

Ja   Jabilo   Jace   Jacey   Jacinda
Jacinta   Jacinth   Jack   Jackie   Jaclyn
Jacob   Jacqueline   Jacquelle   Jacques   Jada
Jade   Jaden   Jadine   Jadon   Jadyn
Jadzia   Jaeger   Jael   Jaelyn   Jafari
Jag   Jagger   Jago   Jai   Jaide
Jailene   Jaime   Jain   Jainna   Jair
Jairo   Jake   Jalen   Jalene   Jalia
Jalil   Jalila   Jam   Jamaica   Jamal
Jamar   Jamarcus   Jame   James   Jamese
Jameson   Jamie   Jamil   Jamir   Jamison
Jamon   Jamya   Jan   Jana   Janae
Jane   Janelle   Janessa   Janet   Janeth
Janette   Janice   Janie   Janika   Janina
Janine   Janis   Janison   Janiya   Janna
January   Janus   Jaquan   Jara   Jarah
Jared   Jaren   Jareth   Jariah   Jarl
Jarlan   Jarmaine   Jaron   Jarrett   Jarvis
Jase   Jaser   Jasmin   Jasmine   Jason
Jasper   Java   Javen   Javier   Javonte
Jax   Jaxon   Jaxton   Jay   Jaya
Jaycee   Jayden   Jaylee   Jayleen   Jaylyn

Jayme   Jayna   Jayne   Jazmine   Jazz
Jazzelle   Jean Jean Baptiste   Jeana Jeanette
Jeanine   Jeanne   Jeb   Jed   Jedi
Jedidiah   Jedrek   Jeff   Jefferson   Jeffery
Jeffrey   Jem   Jemma   Jen   Jena
Jenae   Jenaya   Jenelle   Jeneva   Jenna
Jenner   Jennica   Jennie   Jennifer   Jennis
Jenny   Jennyl   Jensen   Jera   Jered
Jeremiah   Jeren   Jeret   Jeri   Jericho
Jermaine   Jerod   Jerold   Jerome   Jerrell
Jerrin   Jerrod   Jerry   Jerusha   Jesimae
Jess   Jessa   Jesse   Jessenia   Jessia
Jessica   Jessie   Jesus   Jesus   Jethro
Jett   Jetta   Jevonte   Jewel   Jia Li
Jiang   Jie   Jiles   Jill   Jillian
Jimena   Jimmy   Jin   Jira   Jirou
Jiva   Jo   Joachim   Joan   Joanie
Joann   Joanna   Joanne   Job   Jobeth
Jocelin   Jocelyn   Jock   Jody   Joe
Joel   Joelle   Joely   Joey   Johan
Johanna   Johari   John   John   Johnathan
Johnny   Johnson   Joie   Jojo   Jola
Jolanda   Jolie   Jolisa   Jolon   Jon
Jonah   Jonas   Jones   Joni   Jora
Jordan   Jordana   Jorge   Jorja   Jorrin
Jory   Jose   Jose   Josef   Joseph
Joseph   Josette   Josh   Joshua   Josiah
Josie   Joss   Josue   Journey   Jovanna
Jovany   Jovia   Jovie   Jovita   Joy
Joyce   Joylyn   Juan   Juan   Juana
Juanita   Jubal   Jubilee   Juda   Judah
Juda   Judd   Jude   Judge   Judith
Judson   Judy   Jui   Juin   Juji

Juke Jules Julia Julian Juliana Julie Juliet Julio Julisa Julius July Jun June Jung Junior Juniper Junipero Junius Junko Juno Juro Justice Justin Justina Justine Justis Justo Justus Jyoti Jim

Total: 312

K

Kylie - would have loved volleyball and cheerleading. She would have played on Junior Varsity teams throughout her high school career and would have gone on to be an administrative assistant until a handsome young man in a dark suit would have swept her off her feet. They would have married and lived in an older house near the river and raised their two children together. Kylie would have lived an ordinary life. Paid taxes. Loved her grandchildren. Been buried beside her husband in the Presbyterian Cemetery.

Kurt - would have served in the Merchant Marine. A cargo specialist, he would have preferred the relaxed standards of dress to the stricter rules of the Navy he had briefly considered joining. He would have enjoyed motorcycles, and the driveway of his small house would have been perpetually littered with bike parts.

Kevin - would have worked in Hollywood as a greensman. Responsible for the plants and organic material needed to decorate movie sets, he would have developed a broad range of carpentry, masonry, plumbing, and electrical skills which his mother-in-law would have put to good use in her aging home.

Kira - inheriting her father's penchant for collecting stamps, Kira would have had a vast collection, both foreign and domestic, before going to work for the postal service. A lobby clerk in a city branch, rural carrier, and eventual branch manager, Kira would have used her position to encourage budding stamp collectors, even going so far as to speak in local elementary schools about the hobby.

Kim - would have graduated from the Haden Academy of Cosmetology and gone on to specialize in pedicures and waxing. During her life, she would have often worked seven-days a week beside two of her cousins and her aunt, who owned the salon. Back troubles would have sidelined her at the age of forty-two, and she would have spent the next years keeping house for her daughter and grandson.

Katherine - one of the first to recognize the tourism potential of the riverfront in her Mississippi hometown, Katherine would have networked with business-owners, historical societies, and the town council to create a park, open-air market, and tour boat industry there. Her diabetes would have slowed her down in later years, and she would eventually have a foot amputated.

Kay - would have died of SIDS in infancy.

Kaitlyn - would have had her grandmother's spiral curls. What her Mama would have called "a good grade of hair." She would have been born addicted to crack cocaine and spent her early years passing from foster home to foster home until adoptive parents would be found for her. Even there, in a stable environment, she would have struggled and fought as if against her very self. She would have spent the rest of her life in and out of jail for misdemeanors and petty theft.

Kit - would have started off in banking as a junior teller at a local branch office and worked his way up to Senior Loan Officer for the region. His sons would have played soccer, and gone on to become a marriage and family therapist and a public heath social worker. The therapist son would have become mildly famous for successfully treating a celebrity marriage. Kit would have spent his time and a sizable portion of his paycheck renovating old houses, including a Frank Lloyd Wright.

Kary - would have helped children and adults with enuresis overcome their bedwetting. In her twelve years as a 'coach' to them, she would help seven hundred forty-two people learn to stay dry.

These people also died that day. The mother of one of them works near you. Comfort her.

Kadeem   Kai   Kaia   Kailey   Kaipo
Kaira   Kairi   Kaiser   Kaitlyn   Kala
Kale   Kaleigh   Kalil   Kalli   Kamal
Kamana Kamara   Kamber Kame Kamella
Kameron   Kami   Kamil   Kanai   Kane

Kaniesa Kanika Kanta Kara Kyson
Karan Kare Karen Kari Karif
Karin Karina Karinda Karis Karissa
Karisse Karl Karla Karli Karlyn
Karman Karmina Karsen Karsten Kasen
Kasi Kasia Kasim Kaspar Kass
Kassandra Kassia Kassidy Kat Kata
Katalin Katarina Kate Kateisha Katelin
Katelyn Katerina Katherine Kathleen Kathryn
Kathy Katia Katiana Katie Katina
Katlyn Kato Katrice Katriel Katrrina
Katsu Katsuro Katy Katya Kaya
Kayce Kaydence Kayin Kayla Kaylee
Kayleigh Kayley Kaylyn Kayteequa Kaz
Kazuo Kazuyuki Keagan Keaira Keanu
Keaton Kedar Keefe Keefer Keegan
Keely Keen Keena Keenan Keene
Keeran Keesa Keeya Keften Kegan
Kei Keiandra Keiji Keiki Keiko
Keira Keiran Keisha Keith Kelby
Kele Kella Kellan Kelley Kelli
Kellsie Kelly Kellyn Kelsea Kelsey
Kelton Kelvin Kemp Ken Kenan
Kendo Kendale Kendall Kendra Kendria
Kendrick Kendrix Kenisha Kenji Kenley
Kenna Kennan Kennedy Kenneth Kenny
Kensey Kensington Kensley Kent Kenton
Kenya Kenyon Kenzie Keola Keona
Kera Kermit Kern Kerr Kerra
Kerri Kerry Kerryn Keshawn Keshia
Kesia Keto Kevine Kevlyn Keyah
Khalid Khalil Kia Kiana Kiandra
Kiara Kie Kiefer Kieran Kiernan

Kieve Kiki Kiley Kimball Kimber
Kimberly Kimi Kimmy Kina Kindle
King Kingsley Kingston Kinley Kinsey
Kiona Kiora Kipling Kipp Kira
Kiran Kirby Kiril Kirk Kirsten
Kirstie Kiss Kita Kitty Kizzy
Klara Klaus Knight Knox Knute
Ko Kobe Kody Kofi Kojo
Kile Kilton Kong Korbin Kordell
Kori Kris Krish Krishna Krista
Kristen Kristian Kristin Kristina Kristine
Kristopher Kristy Krizia Krystal Kumar
Kwanza Kya Kye Kyla Kylar
Kyle Kylee Kyleigh Kylene Kyler
Kyna Kyra Kyran Kyrie

Total: 275

L

Lily - would have married very young. Too young, by most people's standards, but some people seem to be ready to marry at seventeen, and Lily would have been one of them. In spite of everyone's negative commentary, Lily's first baby would have been well-cared-for and well-raised. Same with the second. She would have been the youngest La Leche League leader in the state when she turned twenty-one. Energetic, and perpetually cute, Lily would have been a great favorite with almost everyone she met, and during her life would have trained and encouraged three hundred twelve different couples through their breastfeeding trials.

Lyle - would have grown up in Boy Scouts, and raised his boys in Boy Scouts, and spent most of his adult life as a Boy Scout Dad, Leader, and regional coordinator for the Jamboree. Even his severely disabled son would have participated, and would have encouraged twenty-one other men to become more involved in the lives of their special needs children.

Lincoln - would have been teased incessantly about his name. The effect would have been made worse because he physically resembled the lanky president. His name would have looked very trendy, however, in the program of the State

Symphony Orchestra, where he would play for more than twenty years as the lead bassoonist.

A clumsy child at "Meet the Instruments" Day would knock the instrument from his hands, where it would break on the floor. Lincoln would have three other bassoons in his home, but never feel comfortable playing on any of them. Two seasons later, Lincoln would leave the orchestra and retire to a coastal Oregon town where he would occasionally write music reviews for the local paper.

Lesley - the son of an English mother and an American father, Lesley, too, would have felt the sting of teasing tongues over his name. He would work as a server at an intensely stressful casino job in Las Vegas before marrying three times, fathering six children, and dying of lung cancer at age forty-nine.

Louelle - A shy girl with glasses from Missouri, Louelle would never have been sure where she belonged. Her mother's family was from inner city St. Louis, and her father was someone who sold his mother drugs. Louelle would have lived with a maternal aunt, and then in foster care. She would have done poorly in school until the teacher suggested her eyesight be evaluated. One state-sponsored eye exam day at the school, Louelle would receive corrective lenses which would change her world overnight. She would have gone on to work in a suburban Walmart, eventually becoming head cashier. Her husband would find her through a mutual friend, and they would spend twenty-two years together before she would have died of breast cancer.

Lola - would have worked for the county government as a clerk in the auditing department for her whole career. When, after thirty-five years of service the budget would be cut and her pension would disappear, Lola would have shared a house with a good friend. They would have enjoyed jazz festivals and museums and once, Lola would have been arrested for being disorderly conduct on a trip to Graceland where she would have climbed onto a wall surrounding the estate, to dance and sing 'Blue Suede Shoes.'

Lucy - would have traveled to northern Europe to learn about her Scandinavian roots. On the trip, she would have met an African man and made a quick decision to marry him. She would eventually regret it, but he would be very pleased with the arrangement. Their children would have been beautiful.

Lakota - would have spent extra time in foster care, as his Native American roots would have prevented a placement with a non-Indian family at a time when no Indian families were available. At fourteen, he would have been emancipated to spare the foster family from further grief at his outspoken and unruly behavior. He would have gone to the Arizona desert and worked in a rural scrap yard.

Lindsay - would have had a stutter. Her mother would have taken her to a mediocre speech therapist who would have done wonders with Lindsay because of the girl's commitment to overcome her speech impediment. Lindsay would have been his star client, and he would have often referred to her at cocktail parties.

Lukas - barrel-chested, with a sarcastic wit, Lukas would have mellowed after ten years as the Fire Marshall in a medium-sized city. He would have played the lottery and won three hundred forty-seven dollars one year, but would have had to hire an accountant to do his taxes, thus negating any positive financial impact of the win.

Laurie - would have been saved by her backpack during a bicycling accident in her teens. Flipping over the handle bars after her front wheel struck a rock at the bottom of a long hill, Laurie would have somersaulted through the air to land on her back. If her slumber party change of clothes had not been inside her pack, she would have broken her back and been paralyzed. As it was, she would have escaped with bruises.

These people also died. Is our Gross National Product lower, since they are gone?

Lacey   Lacole   Lacy   Lada   Ladarius
Laddie   Ladonna   Laina   Laine   Lainey
Laird   Laisha   Lakeisha   Lala   Lalan

LaLana   Lalette   Lali   Lalita   Lalo
Lamar   Lambert   Lamont   Lana   Lanai
Lance   Lancelot   Lander   Landers   Lando
Landon   Landry   Lane   Lang   Langley
Langston   Lani   Lanie   Laquita   Lara
Laraine   Laramie   Larisa   Lark   Larry
Lars   LaShandra   Lassie   Laszlo   Lata
Latanya   Latifah   Latisha   Latoya   Latona
Latrell   Laura   Laura   Laurel   Lauren
Laurence   Laurent   Lavan   Lavanya Lavender
Laverne   Lavey   Lavinia   Lavonne   Lawanda
Lawrence   Lawson   Laxmi   Layla   Lazaro
Lea   Leah   Leala   Leander   Leandro
Leann   Leanna   Lebron   Lee   Leena
Leela   LeGrand   Lei   Leia   Leif
Leigh   Leighanna   Leila   Lela   Len
Lennon   Lennox   Lenora   Leo   Leon
Leona   Leonard   Leonardo   Leone   Leonora
LeQuoia   LeRoy   Lesa   Leslie   Leticia
Letisha   Letitia   Lette   Levi   Levi
Lewis   Lexi   Lexine   Lexis   Leyla
Li Ming   Lia   Liam   Lian   Liana
Liang   Libby   Libba   Liberty   Libra
Lidia   Lila   Lilac   Lilia   Lilianna
Lilith   Lilja   Lilla   Lilli   Lillian
Lilliana   Lilo   Lin   Lina   Linda
Lindsey   Ling   Linore   Liona   Lira
Lisa   Lisandro   Lisbet   Lise   Lissa
Lita   Liubov   Liv   Liv   Livana
Livia   Livingston   Liz   Liza   Lizbeth
Lizzie   LLewellyn   Lloyd   Lluvia   Loa
Loe   Logan   Lois   Loki   Lolita
Lona   London   Lonna   Lonny   Lora

Lorelei Loren Lorena Lorenzo Lorenzo
Loretta Lori Lorna Lotan Lotus
Louis Louanna Louisa Louise Lourdes
Lourdes Love Lowell Lucas Luce
Lucera Lucia Luciano Lucinda Lucretia
Luigi Luis Luis Luke Luke
Lumen Lumina Luna Lupita Luz
Lydia Lyn Lynda Lynn Lynne
Lynton Lyra Lysa Lysander Lytton
Le Li

Total: 238

M

Mercy - would have been born with a withered leg. She would have learned to go about her daily business dragging it behind her, using a crutch for balance. Long struggle and the perpetual difficulty of access would have weathered her into a peaceful, happy, beautiful woman whose smile attracted everyone. She never considered marriage, assuming peacefully that her disability would render her out of contention for a partner.

That same patience would have brought her a man of bodily and spiritual strength who would have loved her, married her, and stayed with her for thirty-four years of marriage. Their two children and seven grandchildren would have bathed in the bright light of Mercy's love for them, and each would have passed the balm of her peaceful demeanor to their own children, grandchildren, godchildren, co-workers, and neighbors.

Magda - would have discovered at age seven that she liked old things. Castles. Books. Languages. She would have studied Latin and Greek and received a classical education culminating with a degree in Canon Law from a Pontifical University in Rome. She would have returned to the United States and worked for the American Bishops in various roles for the rest of her life. Magda would never marry, but chose instead a small nucleus of friends with whom to experience the finer points of North American culture.

Mara - if she had been born, Mara would have had early memories of mountains. She would have learned to hike almost as soon as she could toddle, and would have found her greatest peace among the peaks and valleys of the Ozark mountains. She would have run a small diner famous for bite-sized apple pies and homemade ice cream.

Mike - would have always had a distant affinity for George Washington after reading a biography of the great president who had started his career as a land surveyor in Virginia, a job Mike would have held himself.

Maya - her long, straight golden hair would not have lived up to the coloration of her namesake tribe, but would have made her stand out in a crowd. Often called, "Rapunzel," Maya would have grown it until it reached her feet. All her life, she would love to hear the sharp intake of approving breath which would greet her when she released it from the tortoise shell clips which pinned it neatly to the back of her head. Her children would wrap themselves in it as she held them.

Macon - a businessman and a Southern gentleman, Macon would have run two car dealerships in the outskirts of Mobile. His lots would have been the go-to stores for teenagers looking for their first ride. Macon would have owned Scottish Terriers and shown them at dog shows throughout the South. For eleven years, the Little League team jerseys would have borne the logo of his business, and it was his initial donation which eventually led to the town acquiring an official baseball field complete with bleachers and a scoreboard.

Margie - talkative and outgoing among friends, Margie would have been reticent around strangers and adults. As she became older, the death of her adoptive parents would have left her wondering about her place and purpose in life, increasing her tendency to silence. Margie would have worked in the accounting department of a candy manufacturer as well as two independent accounting firms before retiring to become a full-time grandmother.

Mitchell - would have started in police work and eventually moved to the missing persons investigation office. Through his innovations using social media and online resources, he would be responsible for a great increase in the percentage of missing persons found each year. He would win a cash award at work three years in a row.

These people also died that day. How come we miss people we've never met?

Macarena   Macaulay   Mace   Macy   Madden
Maddox   Madeleine   Madelina   Madison Myrrh

Mae Maeve Magdalena Maggie Magnum
Magnus Mahak Mahalia Mahogany Maho
Mai Maia Maida Maina Maire
Maja Major Makala Malcolm Malcolm
Malik Malinda Malise Mallory Malone
Malvina Mandel Mandisa Mandy Manjit
Manning Manolo Manuel Manuela Manus
Mara Marc Marcel March Marci
Marcia Marcie Marco Marcos Marcus
Marcy Marek Margaret Margarita Marge
Margie Margo Margot Marguerite Mari
Maria Maria Maria Maria Mariah
Mariam Marian Mariana Marianne Maribel
Maribeth Marie Marie Marije Marika
Marlee Marilla Marilyn Marina Mario
Marion Marisa Marisela Marisol Marissa
Marjean Marjorie Mark Mark Mark
Marla Marlene Marley Marquis Marsha
Marshall Marta Martha Martin Martina
Marvela Mary Mary Mary Mary
Maryjane Masako Mason Mateo Matilda
Matt Matteo Matthew Matthew Matthias
Mattie Maura Maureen Maurice Maurus
Mavis Max Maxime Maximilian Maximus
Maxwell Maynard McKenna McKenzie Meaghan
Mecca Media Meena Meg Megan
Meghan Mei Meira Melaney Melanie
Mele Melinda Melissa Melita Melodie
Melvin Mercedes Mercia Meredith Merric
Merrill Merritt Merry Merton Messina
Mia Micah Michael Michael Michael
Michael Michaela Michal Michelle Michelle
Mick Mickey Midori Miguel Miguel

Mika   Mikhail   Milagro   Milagros   Milen
Miles   Miley   Miley   Milo   Mimi
Mina   Minako   Mindy   Minerva   Ming
Minnie   Mio   Mira   Mirabelle   Miracle
Miranda   Miri   Miriam   Missy   Misty
Mitch   Mitchell   Mitsu   Modesto   Modesty
Moe   Mohammed   Moira   Molly   Mona
Monahan   Monica   Monique   Monisha   Monroe
Monserrat   Montague   Monte   Montel   Montezuma
Mora   Morela   Morgan   Moriah   Morley
Morning   Morris   Morrisa   Morrison   Moses
Moshe   Moxie   Moya   Muriel   Murphy
Murray   Mustafa   Mya   Myles   Myra

Total: 248

N

Nancy - would have been the third daughter in a wealthy New England family if her mother's coffee club had not convinced her that two was enough. Dyslexic and lacking the svelte physique of her peers, Nancy would have turned to art for solace. Her grandfather is the curator of an important Boston museum, and Nancy would have developed her drawing, sculpting, and painting skills in the workrooms behind the exhibit halls. In her later years, after marrying and having a son, she would have taken up bookbinding, relishing the sensation of restoring worn treasures for their delighted owners. She would have developed colon cancer and died in her forties, leaving each of her family members to cope in the ways they knew best. Her son would have turned to glass blowing, her husband to serial marriages. Her art students would miss her mentorship terribly.

Nathan - small and slightly built, but strong as a young ox, Nathan would have developed his strength with wood chopping and hauling in his Dad's tree-removal service. His build would have served him well when someone was needed to scale a tree and remove branches. He would have studied engineering and found a job at the same company which gave him an internship. The work would have been moderately interesting, but Nathan would long for life outside the city and would eventually go to teach at a school which incorporated the out-of-doors into its curriculum. Four hundred and seven children would have been influenced by his easy smile and intense concentration. Several would have considered him a greater influence than their parents, and one would have named his first son after him.

Nicole - would have gone by the nickname 'Co-lay,' and would have always looked older than she was. It would have been advantageous in high school, but less beneficial with the passing years. She would have been a photojournalist with a career's worth of New York Times credits to her name. In her free time, Nicole would have run marathons for breast cancer cures in honor of her late friend. Ironically, she herself would have contracted a rare form of breast cancer which she would have overcome.

Norris - would have grown up in a mid-sized city in the Midwest, dropped out of high school, been medically discharged from the Army, and spent the rest of his life driving a bus for the city. He would have been content with his single outstanding achievement: darts champion, for which he would have earned undying glory and recognition at The Stovepipe Inn Bar and Restaurant.

Natashya - daughter of new immigrants to the United States, Natashya would have grown up fluent in English and her parents' native Russian dialect. Balancing between two worlds, Natashya would immerse herself in her studies for escapism and to please her parents, who would want her to succeed at all costs. She would have eventually returned to her parent's homeland and be drafted as an intelligence collector by the latest incarnation of the KGB. All her life, she would have sent small bits of information from her American home and would have been paid enough money to supplement the small salary her home translation business brought in.

Nina - In her sixty-third year, Nina would have been made a simple gesture of kindness to a child. It would have been small enough to go unnoticed by everyone, including herself, but the child's life would have been changed in a slight way. The child would have learned to do small acts of kindness for children, especially hurting children, and in turn, over many decades, would have influenced a small army of children to be thoughtfully kind. The ripples would have spread until the end of time. The child would have brought flowers to Nina's grave every summer.

Natalie - would have had long, stringy brown hair. Her thin, pointed features would not have been beautiful, and she would have struggled under the weight of her Mother's anger all her life. She would have found her way into a life of drugs and multiple husbands until, at age fifty-one, she would have discovered her skill at knotting rosaries through a class in a drug treatment facility. She would have made thousands of rosaries and sent them to every country in the hemisphere. The letters she received in return would have been the brightest lights of her life.

These people also died that day. One of them might have driven past you right now.

Nabila   Nadia   Nadine   Nahla   Naida
Nakita   Nala   Nalani   Nan   Nana
Nanda   Nanette   Nani   Naomi   Napoleon
Nara   Narcissa   Nardo   Nariko   Nash
Natale   Natalia   Natashaly   Nate Nydia
Nathaniel   Nature   Nautica   Navarro Naveed
Neal   Ned   Neema   Neil   Nella
Nellie   Nellis   Nelson   Nen   Nena
Neo   Neona   Nerissa   Nessa   Nestor
Neva   Nevan   Neville   Newman   Newton
Nia   Niara   Nicholai   Nicholas   Nick
Nicki   Nicklaus   Nicky   Nico   Nicola
Nicolas   Nida   Nieve   Nigel   Night
Nika   Nikita   Nikki   Niko   Nikolai
Nils   Niran   Nisa   Nita   Nixie
Noa   Noah   Noe   Noel   Noelle
Noella   Noemi   Nola   Nolan   Noland
Nona   Noor   Nora   Norah   Noralie
Norbert   Noreen   Nori   Norm   Norma
Norman   Normandie   Noura   Nouvel   Nova
Novak   Novia   Nuala   Nuncio   Nura
Nuren   Nuri   Nuria

Total: 115

O

Ophelia - would have been born to a university student and her literature professor. She would have lived with her emotionally-distant grandparents while her mother finished school, and met her father only once. Ophelia would try acting, singing, and dancing. She would try to be a chef, a doula, and personal assistant. When she no longer would be able to hold together the gaping wounds inside her heart, she would have her own daughter, and would take a job as a secretary which she would hold onto long enough to meet the electrician who came to fix the air conditioner. They would marry and keep on trying to make it work. When death would finally part them, twenty-four years later, Ophelia would have been a happier woman, from the daily small doses of love purified by endurance, which her marriage provided.

Otto - a business columnist for a regional website, Otto would have traveled extensively. While interviewing a financial officer at a local IT company, he would have slipped on a carpet runner and fallen down a flight of stairs. Three surgeries later, his torn knee ligaments would still not function properly, and he would have to tape and brace the joint for the rest of his life. Otto would have enjoyed flying model airplanes in competitions throughout the country. His colleagues would have joked that he would never marry, because any cute little airplane turned his head. He would have, in fact, remained single all his life.

Orson - would have been born to his high-school-junior Mom, who would have carried him on her hip to every school activity, regardless of the stares and muted laughter which often followed her. She would have seen him safely through school, even though it meant she could not do all the fun teenage and young adult activities which seemed to consume her peers. She would have instilled in him a strong faith which she discovered in her early twenties, and he would have made her proud when he graduated from trade school with a journeyman's card as an electrician. He would have moved to master electrician and eventually married, supporting his family and his mother by starting a general contracting business.

Octavian - would have been called "Doc Oc" by his friends, and would have played on a high school All-Star basketball team three years running. A car accident would have ruined his chances at a college scholarship, so Octavian would have gone into sales, where his friendly smile and six-foot-three frame would have garnered him recognition and accomplishment.

Ortega - would have followed in his family's footsteps - a bathtub refinishing business when there were clients, and a catering truck when there were not. He would have married a freshly arrived immigrant from Honduras named Assunta, and they would have had three kids before Assunta's health failed. His children would have followed him into construction trades, and the proudest day of his life would have been the one when his 'Ortega and Sons' business cards arrived in the mail.

Onna - was eleven weeks pregnant when she went to the Oakhaven Women's Center for an elective abortion. At 12:48, the doctor perforated her uterus as he dissected Jagger and scraped his placenta from her body. Onna bled profusely, but was not transported to Manpasset General. Instead, she was sent home in her boyfriend's car with four extra sanitary pads and instructions to go to the Emergency Room if the bleeding didn't stop within twenty-four hours. She died from blood loss and sepsis at 7:17 PM.

These people also died that day. So much joy, missed.

Oakley Odelia Odessa Odette Odin
Obama Odo Odysseus Ogden Ojai
Oberon Ojal Ojas Oke Oksana
Ocean Ola Olaf Olathe Ole
Octavio Oleg Olesia Olga Oliana
Odele Olinda Olisa Oliva Olive
Odelle Oliver Olivia Olivier Ollie
Olson Olympia Oma Omar Omana
Omar Omega Omer Omri Ona
Oneill Onofre Onslow Oona Opa

Opal   Oprah   Ora   Oran   Oren
Oral   Orestes   Oriana   Orien   Orion
Orlando   Orleans   Orma   Ormand   Oro
Orrin   Orsino   Orville   Osborn   Osias
Osma   Osmond   Ossie   Oswald   Othello
Otis   Ovidio   Oxford   Oya

Total: 84

P

Petra - would have been a history buff. She would have especially loved the Civil War, and, as her mother would have lived in Washington, DC, she would have been able to visit historical sites and participate in re-enactments, soaking up information until she herself would have been hired by a local historical society to teach groups of school children.

Prissy - would have struggled with her weight. As a child, she would always have been called "chubby." As an adult, the weight of her failing marriage and the needs of her children and her job would have driven her into the arms of food for solace. Finally, at three hundred twenty-one pounds, her insurance would have paid for surgery to reduce the size of her stomach, and although it wouldn't solve the problem, it would help. Prissy would enjoy the novelty of going to the grocery store without frowning, disgusted looks from fellow shoppers, and kind treatment from strangers, rather than averted eyes.

Paul - raised in a suburban neighborhood by adoptive parents, Paul would have excelled in school. He would have been admitted to a good state college and graduated with a degree in business accounting. He would have earned a place at Vanguard as a financial service provider working directly with clients. He would not enjoy it, and would transfer to a division of the company where he could work all day with numbers. His son would have enjoyed wrestling and biking, and Paul would have coached his daughter's soccer team. His grandson would have showed similar prowess with numbers and grandfather and grandson would have spent long Saturday afternoons solving complex arithmetic problems while the boy's grandmother plied them with baloney sandwiches and iced tea.

Peter - always sensitive to the changing moods of his unstable mother, Peter would have thrived in the stability of his first foster home. When a permanent placement would be found for him, Peter would regret not being able to stay with his foster mother, a regret which would lead to anger and conflict. Emancipated at seventeen, Peter would find work in the shipyards, and would marry twice. When his second wife started going to Church, he would join her and eventually be baptized. He would be the go-to man in his neighborhood for any mechanical difficulty and would hold weekly Bible studies in his home.

Preston - would have loved airplanes. Assigned a 'Big Brother' in an after-school program, Preston would have expressed his desire to fly and have been taken to the local airfield by the Big Brother. Trouble in school would have lead to his quitting early and a stint in the county jail. Inspired by brochures in the education office of the jail,

Preston would join the Air Force and learn to repair airplane engines. Eventually, he would save enough money to buy and restore an old Cessna, earn his pilot's license, and spend his weekends flying and teaching cadets in the Civilian Air Patrol.

Pandora - would have been born with severe Fetal Alcohol Syndrome and lived in a state-run facility all of her forty-three years.

Pablo - the third child born to his inattentive mother, Pablo would have been victimized by an uncle and lost in the homosexual underground of his city. He would have died from severe intestinal problems at age sixteen.

Porter - would have been adopted by parents who did not know of his existence until they received a phone call one morning saying he was available. Loved fiercely by his new parents, Porter would have enjoyed every possible advantage. At fourteen, he and his father would have contacted his birth parents and shared an unfulfilling afternoon with each of them. He would go on to become an adoption advocate and speak widely on the subject throughout the country. At his suggestion, a state senator would sponsor a bill easing adoption requirements at the county level.

These people also died that day. Who will pay down the national debt?

Paco   Paddington   Padgett   Padma   Page

Paige   Paiva   Palma   Palmer   Paloma
Pam   Pamela   Pancho   Pansy   Paola
Paolo   Paquita   Parees   Paresh   Paris
Parisa   Park   Parker   Parrish   Parson
Parvani   Pascal   Pascale   Pascual   Pasha
Passion   Pat   Patia   Patience   Paton
Patrice   Patricia   Patrick   Patrick   Patsy
Patty   Paula   Paulette   Paulina   Pauline
Paulo   Paulos   Pavel   Pax   Paxton
Payton   Pax   Paz   Peace   Peaches
Peanut   Pearl   Pebbles   Pedro   Peer
Peggy   Pelagia   Pele   Pello   Pelton
Pemberley Pembroke Penelope   Penn   Penney
Pennie   Penny   Pepper   Percival   Percy
Perdita   Peregrine   Peri   Perlita   Perpetua
Perrin   Perry   Pete   Petit   Petula
Phalen   Phil   Philip   Phillipa   Philomena
Phobe   Phuc   Phuong   Phyllis   Pia
Pier   Pierce   Pierre   Piers   Pieta
Pilar   Ping   Piotr   Pippa   Piri
Pixie   Placido   Plato   Polly   Ponce
Pooja   Porfirio   Porsche   Portia   Posh
Potter   Powell   Pranav   Pravar   Precia
Precious Prentice   Prescott Presencia Presley
Price   Primavera   Prince   Prita   Priti
Priya   Prosper   Pryce   Psyche   Peyton

Total: 143

Q

Quentin - would have always been in trouble as a child. Raised in a small apartment in the middle of a bad part of Baltimore, he would have had no where to expend his copious energy. Left alone for many of his non-school hours, he would soon have become acquainted with the police department. Finally sent to juvenile detention, Quentin would have failed his English classes but shown great skill in math.

By chance, he would be offered a class in computer programming, and taught by a crazy, skeletally-thin man who would have completely understood Quentin's restless energy. The instructor would have allowed Quentin complete freedom of movement in the computer lab, and the boy would have created intricate and beautiful computer programs while, standing, jumping, and rolling on the floor.

With some help from summers in the country and stabilizing medication, Quentin would have been granted a student internship with the National Security Agency and soon would have received a job offer. He would have spent his entire life working for "the Agency," collecting twenty-one patents for his groundbreaking computer work.

Quill - an artist and writer, Quill would have loved the dramatic arts and eventually become a reporter for a large public radio network. His paintings would have been less popular, and at his yearly gallery show, only his grandparents would have purchased his works. These, they would have kept wrapped in sheets in their basement.

Quinn - the last child of highly creative but financially challenged parents, Quinnie would have struggled to fit in. Everything about her would have been average, and as she wouldn't have liked the graphic arts which absorbed her parents and older siblings, she would have turned to cheerleading, shopping, and long telephone conversations with her friends. She would marry her high school sweetheart and work for awhile as a customer service representative for a home construction business before having two children of her own, whom she would have named Katie and Joey.

These people also died that day. Their grandparents think about them all the time.

Qi Qing   Quade   Quang   Queenie
Quenby   Quentin   Querida   Quetzal Quito
Quilla   Quincy   Quinta   Quintin   Quinto
QuiQui   Quita

Total: 20

R

Ramon - his mother is an undocumented hispanic laborer in Denver. Pregnant for the second time in a year, she was overwhelmed, and used her savings to "take care of it."

Ramon would have been adopted through a religious organization who would have also provided his mother with a home, had she known. He would have grown up in a suburban neighborhood, raised by his professional adopted parents. Although there would have been little more than his looks to identify him as hispanic by the time he graduated from high school, he would have been greatly interested in his biological roots, and would have become involved with local hispanic organizations, where, ironically, he would have begun to learn Spanish.

Rafael - the child of hispanic teenagers, initially, his existence would have brought tears and screams of frustration from his grandparents, first-generation immigrants from Nicaragua. By the time he would have been born, however, he would have been well-loved and much anticipated.

He would have been spoiled and obese by the time he was old enough for Kindergarten, but would have lost much of the weight when he grew enough to play soccer. His dream would have been to play in the World Cup, and although he never would, he would avidly follow the competition his whole life. He would have become an altar boy, and in his later years, a deacon in his Church, where his well-padded figure would have been a fixture at Church events.

Rachel - tall and lithe, Rachel's easy smile and long, wavy hair would have made her popular, if never pretty. Endowed with a good singing voice and an outgoing personality, she would have played lead roles in her school drama program, and would have even landed a role in a production in college, before her veterinary studies consumed her. Three years into college, she would have dropped out to elope with a man nearly twice her age. She would have spent many years working part-time to pay off her college debts, and have divorced and remarried twice. Her second son would have been a technical assistant in a recording studio, eventually making his way to Nashville where he would become a producer at a lesser-known record label.

Randall - 'Randy,' as his adoptive parents would have called him, would have become a lawyer at a small firm in Indianapolis where he would begin his career working with small-claims litigation and eventually move into family law. He would advertise his practice on billboards and in the phone book, and his catchy radio ads would make him locally recognizable to an entire generation in central Indiana.

Reina - would have been born at a free hospital for poor mothers, and have grown up fatherless supported by welfare, food stamps, public school, and a dedicated Mom. Reina would join a free class which would teach her to be a Licensed Practical Nurse, and would have spent the next nine years working with the elderly in nursing homes around the county. Eventually, she would earn a Bachelor's of Nursing degree and become the director of the Licensed Practical Nurses' training program. She and her husband would have three boys, all of whom would go into medicine. The youngest, Carlos, would make it all the way through medical school and specialize in geriatric oncology.

Rex - loud, energetic, and an excellent teacher, Rex would have taken advantage of a program which paid for his education in exchange for several years of inner-city teaching. His joy and enthusiasm for kids and learning would have made him into a magnet for hurting children, and he would have won several 'Teacher of the Year" awards during his thirty-eight year career. At his funeral, they would have had an overflow crowd, and ten years after his death, his widow would have continued to receive letters from former students expressing their gratitude for the influence Rex had on their lives.

Richard - would have joined the Army at seventeen to get away from a messy home life.

Sent to a hotspot two-weeks after graduating from Basic Training, "Rich" would have lost his life in a suicide-bombing attack. His mother would have been the beneficiary of his life insurance policy and used nearly all of it to bury him properly.

Rudy - would have been born "Rudolph," but because of a deer similarly monikered, he would have gone by Rudy his whole life. One arm shorter than the other, Rudy would have learned early how to use his good arm in the fastest right hook in his grade. After his sixteenth birthday, he would have left home and school and drifted until drunk and homeless, he would have been picked up by a ministry for homeless young men. Six months later, clean and sober, Rudy would have been permitted to assist on his first film shoot - a public service announcement contracted to the homeless shelter which teaches the young men to work in film.

Twenty years and seven motion pictures later, Rudy would have been a major name in Indie films on the East Coast. He would have used his minor celebrity to create awareness about the plight of homeless teens, and raise funds for the shelter which had rescued him. His wife and twin daughters would never meet his parents.

Radar - born to a college student, Radar would have been adopted by fans of TV's "M*A*S*H," and although officially named Fredrick, he would have been known as Radar by friends and family. A Cub scout and Boy Scout, Radar would have earned his Eagle Scout at fifteen by constructing a gazebo in a local park. He would have learned the retail business from his Dad, who ran a franchise hardware store, and by the time he was forty, he would have owned twelve stores in the greater St. Louis area.

Radha - would have flown effortlessly through school, following the wishes of her recently arrived and more recently married parents to become a doctor. She would have been accepted to medical school, but transferred to Art school. Unwilling to support her in an occupation in which they could see no practical value, Radha's parents would have given her an ultimatum: return to medical school or be cut off from the family. She would have reluctantly returned to medical school and become a pediatric rheumatologist, putting her art to work in beautiful murals which would adorn the walls of her practice, and encouraging her patients to express themselves artistically.

Ronald - born with Trisomy-18 disorder, Ronald would have lived for forty-five minutes, and have been buried with ceremony, a name, and gravestone, allowing his family to grieve.

These people also died that day. What is the value of a single human life?

Racquel Radley   Raeanne   Raffaello Raheem
Rahm   Rahul   Raimi   Rain   Raisa
Raith   Rajan   Raleigh   Ralph   Ram

Ramona Ransey Randi Ranger Ranjeet
Rashad Rashid Raul Raven Ravi
Ray Raymundo Read Reagan Reba
Rebecca Rebekah Reda Redford Ree
Reece Reed Reese Reeves Regina
Reginald Regis Reid Reign Reilly
Remi Remus Renata Rene Renee
Reuben Reuel Revonda Rey Reyna
Rhett Rhianna Rhiannon Rhonda Rhys
Ricardo Richelle Rico Rider Ridge
Riki Riley Rimona Rina Rio
Rissa Rita River Riyaz Rizzo
Roald Rob Robbin Robert Robert
Roberto Robin Robyn Rocio Rocky
Rod Roderick Rodney Rodolfo Roger
Roja Rolando Rolf Rollo Roma
Roman Romano Romeo Ron Ronald
Ronaldo Ronda Rong Ronni Ronnie
Rory Rosa Rosa Rosalia Rosalie
Rosanna Rosario Roscoe Rose Roseanne
Roselyn Rosemarie Rosemary Rosetta Roshaun
Rosie Rosina Rosita Ross Rowan
Roxanna Roxanne Roxy Roy Royal
Royce Ruana Ruben Ruby Rue
Ruhan Rumer Ruri Russ Russell
Rusti Ruth Ryan Ryann Rupert
Rylan Rylee Ryo Ryosuke Ryoto
Ryu Ramiro Rosalind Ryder

Total: 165

S

Samantha - would have been adopted by a large family. She would have been the baby, and much doted upon. Shimmering, thigh-length blond/brown hair would have been her trademark, along with her outgoing personality, and hysterical laugh. Samantha would have married Rob, who she knew in elementary school, and they would have had twelve children, forty-three grandchildren, and enough great-grands to populate a small town. Known as "Grammy" to everyone who wasn't her child, Samantha's words and actions would have been replicated through generations of family, enough to change the entire character of Prince Fredrick County, Maryland in the Twenty-First century.

Unfortunately, the woman who usually stood outside the Women's Health Clinic where Samantha died, did not come that morning with her sign offering help to pregnant woman, and was not there to offer a word of encouragement to Samantha's mother, who was experiencing second thoughts. It would have only been a short exchange, the woman offering Samantha's mom the option of adoption and a friendly smile, but that morning, she slept late after watching the Academy Awards the night before, and decided no harm would come from missing her monthly appointment in front of the clinic.

Sha'Ree - would have been born into an abusive family with little ambition and fewer resources. Raised by the television and public schools, Sha'Ree would have known little of the world beside the loud voice necessary to get what she needed, be it food, attention, or affection.

By age fourteen, she would have had a child of her own and have been facing misdemeanor charges for minor theft. By eighteen, she would be incarcerated for theft and drug charges. In prison, she would make some effort toward a high school equivalency degree, but without a support system on the outside, she would soon fall back into the same lifestyle, making the same choices her mother and her grandmother made. Sha'Ree would die of an overdose of heroin at twenty-six.

Stefan - knowing the value of a good set of clothes, Stefan would have styled his way into the lives of women for his living. An impeccable dresser, he would insure his closet contained up-to-date looks via the credit cards of the working women he dated. He would be many years in this lifestyle, hopping from one woman to another before finally landing in jail for credit card fraud. He would be in and out of jail for the rest of his life.

Shanna - a love of books, especially picture books, would have led Shanna into a career at a chain bookseller. After several months as a cashier, she would have become a manager of the night shift, overseeing the store as it closed, restocked, and completed the accounting for the day. Even when she married and had her three children, she would continue to work with books. Moving to the day shift to accommodate the kids' schedules, Shanna would eventually become manager of the entire store, and the author of her own unsuccessful picture book.

Suzy - would have developed leukemia at age six and spent her remaining two years in the Children's Hospital in Salt Lake City. An overdose of radiation would have destroyed her lungs, and she would have died within hours. Her funeral would have been held at Brigham Young university, and a student who heard about her would have been inspired to enter medicine and become a pediatric oncologist.

Scott - a baseball player and Naval Academy graduate, Scott would never master personal hygiene at the level considered socially acceptable. In his later years, still single, he would put on considerable weight and have heart problems.

Siobhan - True to her Irish heritage, Siobhan would have played the harp and sung beautifully as a child. She would have put a music career on hold to marry and have a family and never get back to it, except to encourage her children to express their own music. One of her children would play concert piano, one would build houses, and one was happiest working with stone. He would have become a well-known stone mason who specialized in rebuilding stone walls, dressing foundation stones, and creating traditional Irish stone houses.

Sanders - an encyclopedic knowledge of American history would have set Sanders apart from the boys his age who played with video games and Legos. He would earn scholarships to his choice of colleges, and a Ph.D. in history before age thirty. Traveling the lecture circuit and a busy schedule as a professor and consultant for films, he would have never married, instead, channeling his energy into a highly successful foundation for the preservation of traditional American culture.

These people also died that day. Imagine the emotional condition of an abortion nurse.

Saba   Sabina   Sabrina   Sadie   Sage
Sally   Salvador   Sam   Sameya   Sampson
Samuel   Sancho   Sanders   Sandra   Sandro
Sanford   Sanjay   Sanjeet   Santa   Santiago
Santo   Sara   Sapphire   Sarah   Saran
Sari   Sasha   Satin   Saul   Savanna
Sawyer   Sayer   Scarlett   Schuyler   Scout
Seamus   Sean   Sebastian   Seiko   Sellas
Selby   Selena   Selene   Selma   Sephora
Sequoia   Serenity   Sereno   Sergio   Seth
Severino   Shakila   Shakir   Shana   Shanae
Shandra   Shannon   Shanti   Shaquille   Sharell

Sharif Sharlene Sharon Shaun Shauna Shawn Shay Shaya Shayla Shayna Shea Sheba Sheela Sheena Sheila Shelby Sheldon Shelley Sheng Shep Sheridan Sherine Sherise Sherlyn Sherman Sherri Sherrill Sherry Sheryl Shiloh Shin Shinjiro Shirley Shiva Shona Shoshana Sibyl Sicily Sidney Sienna Sierra Sigfried Sigourney Sigrid Silas Silver Silvestre Silvia Sima Simon Simone Sincerity Sinclair Sinead Siri Sissy Skipper Sky Skylar Sofia Sojourner Sol Solana Soledad Solomon Sona Sonia Sonja Sonny Sonya Sophia Sophie Soren Sorina Spence Spencer Spiro Stacey Stacia Stacie Stacy Stan Stanford Stanislaw Stanko Stanley Stanton Star Stasia Stavros Stedman Stefan Stefanie Stefanos Steffi Stella Stephan Stephanie Stephen Sterling Steve Steven Stevie Stewart Stormy Stuart Suave Subira Sue Sugar Sullivan Sumana Summer Suna Sunny Suri Susan Susanna Susannah Susanne Susie Suzanne Suzette Symona Svana Sybil Sydney Sylvester Sylvia Sylvie

Total: 198

T

Trish - would have grown up in Eastern Washington state, riding with her grandfather, a rancher, up and down the hills and valleys. She would have spent a lot of time alone, and along with a compassionate heart for troubled creatures, Trish would have had a tendency toward obesity. She would have studied astronomy at Washington State University.

Moving to Seattle for a job, Trish would despise the weather and come home to care for her aging grandparents and work in a dental office. Trish would have inherited her grandparent's ranch and tried unsuccessfully to turn a profit. Finally, she would have given up and hired a manager to take care of it. They would have married and enjoyed an amicable relationship until lung cancer would take him. Trish would have sold the ranch and moved into an apartment in town, teaching astronomy at the Senior Center.

Tomas - would have been born to recent immigrants who had lived in the mountains of southern Mexico. He would have been drawn to high altitudes and have become a National Park ranger, enjoying equally his assignments in Arkansas, Virginia, and Alaska. A run-in with a drunken park visitor on a snowmobile would leave him with a limp. Tomas would have retired with a dozen awards and lived out his life in a remote cabin in the Cascade mountain range.

Tasha - would have been born without a left ear and have been subjected to four reconstructive surgeries before her seventh birthday. The difference in her anatomy in no way would have affected her intellect, however. Tasha would have earned a scholarship to a prestigious prep school and gone on to one of the best colleges in the south. After a decade in tax law, she would have stayed home to raise her four children. Instead of going back to law, Tasha would have written and illustrated children's books about heroes of her state, none of which would have sold well.

Tara - abused and broken by her teenaged, emotionally-crippled mother, Tara would have been adopted by the sister of a neighbor. In spite of therapy and reconstructive surgery to repair her damaged torso, Tara would not be able to cope with the everyday responsibilities of life, eventually dying of pneumonia on the streets of San Jose.

Timoteo - would have shown an affinity for helping rehabilitated criminals during his years as a beat cop on the Boston Police force. He would have trained as a parole officer, where he would have worked for twenty-two years, six in Boston and sixteen in Natick, where his older son would have been killed in a street fight. Two months later, he would have retired from the police force and spent the majority of his remaining life speaking to youth in area schools about the dangers of violence.

Trent - would have been a night watchman at four different culturally significant buildings in Philadelphia before being stabbed in the back early one May morning. He would have spent two years in rehab.

Tabitha - would have done very little with her life or her latent organizational abilities. She would have sat on the couch watching television and entertaining male visitors, just as her mother would have taught her.

These people also died that day. Who will do the good they would have done?

Tadeo   Tahira   Tai   Taigi   Taini
Tait   Tala   Talbot   Talen   Talia
Talisa   Talise   Talisha   Tallis   Tallulah
Talon   Tamal   Tamara   Tamarice   Tamar
Tambika   Tameka   Tamera   Tammy   Tamra
Taneisha   Tania   Tanika   Tanner   Tanya
Taran   Tarin   Tariq   Taryn   Tasheika
Tate   Tatiana   Tatum   Tavaril   Tavia
Tawana   Tay   Taya   Tayden   Tayla
Taylor   Teagan   Teague   Ted   Teela
Tegan   Teige   Teigra   Teisha   Tejana
Telissa   Tendai   Teneil   Teo   Teofila
Terence   Teresa   Terra   Terrel   Terrell
Terrence   Terri   Terrica   Terry   Teryl
Tessa   Teva   Tex   Thad   Thai

Thalassa Thalia Thao Thatcher Thelma
Theodore Theone Thera Theresa Therese
Theresia Thom Thomae Thomas Thorne
Thornton Thuong Thurman Thuy Tia
Tiana Tien Tiernan Tierney Tierra
Tiffany Tiger Tikvah Tilda Tilden
Tillie Tim Timothy Tino Tiona
Tira Tiran Tito Tobias Toby
Todd Toki Tomai Tomiko Tommy
Tomoya Toni Tonia Tony Tonya
Topper Toren Tori Torrance Torrell
Toya Trace Tracey Traci Tracy
Trang Tranquila Trapper Travis Trevor
Trey Treyvon Tricia Trinity Tripp
Trisha Tristan Trixie Troy Trudy
Truman Trumble Truong Trygg Tryn
Tu Tuan Tucker Tudor Twila
Twyla Ty Tyler Tylie Tyne Tyshawn
Tyra Tyran Tyree Tyrell Tyrone Tyson

Total: 179

U

Una - long, dark brown wavy hair, clear bronze complexion, flashing white teeth, and a complementary figure would have opened many doors for Una. Her mother would have done her best to protect her from the inevitable opportunists which would have crawled over one another for the chance to sign Una to a modeling contract. In the end, she would have gone to college by way of low key modeling shoots for regional companies, and only with a Bachelor's in biology would she have taken larger jobs.

Despite her mother's warnings, Una would have fallen into some of the ugly habits of the fashion industry, rescued only by Multiple Sclerosis, which removed her from the runway. With no pressure to keep up her looks, Una worked for the Monterey Bay Aquarium as the enterprise's public face while pursuing higher education in marine biology. She would eventually marry, but be unable to have children, a secret pain lost on many who hated her for the seeming ease of life provided by her physical beauty.

V

Victoria - an illegitimate child in a strictly traditional Japanese family, Victoria would not have been a stranger to pressure. Her grandparents would have had little to do with her mother or the American Jew who fathered her, but they would have required perfection in academics, music, and art. In reality, Victoria was wonderfully gifted on the violin, but she would never learn to love the instrument because of the stress it represented.

A straight A student, she would have graduated from Harvard with a dual physics/fine arts degree, but completely burned out, she would have become ill and unable to work for seven years, during which time her rising star would have faded, her grandmother would have passed away, and she would again feel strong enough to make her way through life, teaching physics and violin at a private high school in San Francisco.

W

Walter - would have lived into his forties as a mid-level manager at a textile manufacturing mill in South Carolina before meeting Joni, a health inspector with a thick Southern drawl who would have come to see the mill. When Walter would have married her a year later, they would have been happy. They would have welcomed three children, and learned Polka dancing, competing in regional competitions throughout the South. Because Walter died before his own birth, however, Joni instead married a car salesman, had one child with autism, and chain smoked, dying of lung cancer at fifty-two, never having heard of the Polka.

X

Xavier - would have traveled extensively as an entertainer for a cruise ship line based out of Fort Lauderdale. Because no one on a cruise ship ever has just one job, he would have also tended bar and acted as a french translator whenever his services were needed.

At the end of his career, he would have sailed all seven seas, helped with disaster relief and natural disaster evacuations on two occasions, had four sexually transmitted diseases, and fathered six children, three of whom would never have known his name.

Y

Yesenia - would have been born of a woman who crossed the Sonoran Desert barefoot to come to the United States. Possessing her mother's strength of will, Yesenia was actually born alive after the abortion, but the nurse bundled her into the medical waste container with the other remnants of her mother's pregnancy, where she died.

Z

Zana - would have been known to the world as the little girl on YouTube singing a love song to her mother. The video would have had more than nineteen million hits and have spawned dozens of spin-offs. A doll with a recording of her song would have become a popular Mothers' Day gift in the United States.

These people also died that day. Is it right to choose to snuff out a life for my own convenience?

Udell Ugo Ula Ulema Ulf
Ulric Ulysses Uma Umberto Ume
Umi Unique Unity Upton Ura
Urbano Uriel Urja Usher Uzuri
Val Valene Valentina Valerie Valeri
Valiant Valdo Van Vance Vanessa
Vanna Vanya Varda Varian Vasanti
Vasily Vaughan Vega Velma Velvet
Venetia Venturo Venus Vera Verdad
Verdi Verity Verna Verona Veronica
Vi Vicente Vicki Vicky Victor
Vida Vienna Viggo Vijay Viktor
Villette Vince Vincent Viola Violet
Virginia Vittorio Viveca Vivian Viviana
Vivienne Vladimir Von Vonte Veronique
Walden Walker Wallace Ward Warner
Warren Waseem Washington Watt Waverly
Wayne Webb Wells Wendy Weston
Wheatley Whitney Willa Willard Willem
William William Willis Willow Wilson
Winfield Winifred Winona Winston Winthrop
Wolf Woodrow Worth Wright Wyatt
Wynn Wynne Wade Xanadu Xantho
Xenia Xenon Xia Xiang Xing
Xena Yaal Yaeger Yan Yankee
Yardley Yas Yaser Yasmin Yassah
Yates Ye Yehuda Yo Yoko
Yolanda Yori York Yosef Yoshi
Yoshiko Yousef Yu Yul Yulia
Yuri Yves Yvette Yanni Zacchaeus
Zachary Zack Zahra Zaila Zaire
Zamora Zander Zandra Zara Zebedeo
Zeena Zeke Zena Zenia Zeshawn

Zevi Zhen Zia Zita Zoe
Zola Zona Zora Zorina Zoya
Zulu Zuri Zechariah

Total: 184

Three thousand, eight hundred seventy-seven lives lost.

An unspeakable horror which will be repeated tomorrow.

And the next day.

And the next.

Who will stop it?

postlude

So many questions.

Why do we allow abortion to continue?

Why do we think people are a problem, rather than the solution? Why don't we see people as the source of ideas which will provide far more resources than they will consume?

Why do some insist the loss of our population and all their descendants is really none of our business?

Why pretend there are no long-term effects?

I don't know.

I do know members of my own family are not here today because of abortion.

I miss them.

Made in the USA
Columbia, SC
15 September 2022